Contents

CW01433518

Chapter 1: January.............................1
*Why Run? We explore the purpose and benefits of
running in our lives.*

Chapter 2: February..........................13
*Finding rhythm, understanding pace, cadence,
and the importance of consistency.*

Chapter 3: March 23
*From mindset to miles. Developing a runner's
mindset and mental toughness.*

Chapter 4: April 36
*Fueling your passion. Nutrition, hydration,
and the importance of fueling your runs.*

Chapter 5: May................................50
*The power of community, building connections
with fellow runners and joining local groups.*

Chapter 6: June 66
*Embracing the great outdoors and exploring the
joys of running in nature and different terrains.*

Chapter 7: July 79
*Recovery and Resilience, Importance of rest,
recovery techniques, and preventing injuries.*

Chapter 8: August............................95
*Setting goals and breaking barriers. How to
set achievable goals and push your limits.*

Chapter 9: September........................ **110**

*Running through Life's challenges, using running
as a tool for coping with stress and adversity.*

Chapter 10: October **130**

*The runner's journey, exploring personal growth
and the transformative power of running.*

Chapter 11: November........................ **146**

*Celebrating successes. reflecting on
achievements and milestones, big or small.*

Chapter 12: December........................ **162**

*Running into the future. Setting intentions for the
coming year and the lifelong journey of running.*

WHY RUN?
WHAT IT MEANS FOR US

PHYSICAL
HEALTH

MENTAL
CLARITY

EMPOSTAL
BALANCE

PURPOSE

CONNECTION
TO SELF & NATURE

JANUARY

Chapter 1:
JANUARY

Why Run? We explore the purpose and benefits of running in our lives.

Seasonal Reflection:

As winter envelops the earth, the world feels quieter. The crisp air stimulates your senses and reminds you of the fresh start the New Year brings.

Mindfulness Theme:

Embrace the stillness of January as a time for introspection. Focus on your breath while running, using the cold air to ground you and awaken the present moment.

Mental Health Insight:

The post-holiday lull can induce feelings of sadness or lethargy. Observe how the act of running boosts your endorphins, helping you combat winter blues and setting a positive tone for the year ahead.

January Mantra:

"I run to remember who I am, to feel the ground beneath me, and to rise with every step."

Why Run? What It Means for Us

Before the medals or the shoe companies, before the miles tracked on apps, before the high-tech weather wicking clothing and shiny race bibs, there was always the simple, sacred act of running. No music, no finish lines, no race t-shirts. Just heartbeat, breath and earth. Running is not a new trend invented to support the growth in social media or to make us look cool. This is a return, a return to something deeply human, something wired into our genetics, something stirring in our bones.

This chapter is an invitation to delve deeper and explore further. To understand why we run, not just with our legs but with our history, our health, and our hope. Whether you're lacing up for the first time or rekindling a long-lost fire, this isn't just about fitness. It's about discovery, rediscovery and reconnection. I would go so far to say, it's an opportunity for us to take the first steps together in figuring out how to rewild our spirit.

Running is a legacy in Our DNA, long before running was a race, it was a reason, an essential survival skill that shaped the very course of human evolution. Our ancestors didn't run for medals; they ran for meals, for survival and I am not talking about racing to McDonald's before it closes. Picture them racing across the vast open savannas, chasing down prey and relying on sheer endurance to outlast animals that could easily outrun them in speed. Scientists refer to this technique as persistence hunting, but it was more than just a hunting method; it was a vital means of existence.

Our bodies are literally built to run. The anatomy of the human form tells a story of evolutionary adaptation that favors endurance. Our Achilles tendons act like springs, offering elasticity and energy efficiency (though at my age it doesn't always feel like it), while our glutes which are among the most powerful muscles in the body, provide the necessary force for long-distance movement. Additionally, our ability to sweat, a critical adaptation that cools our bodies during exertion, offers us a remarkable advantage in endurance activities.

Each time you lace up your shoes and hit the ground, you're not just exercising; you're waking up ancient instincts that lie dormant. With every stride, you honor generations of humans who ran before you, not on sanitized rubber tracks, but across rugged terrain and under open skies. When you run, you engage in an act that connects you to your ancestry, embracing the legacy of those who relied on running for survival, exploration, and connection to their world.

Running is not merely a physical activity; it's a manifestation of our heritage. It's a celebration of the triumphs of our ancestors and an acknowledgment of the skills and attributes that have been passed down through millennia. In essence, running is not just something we do; it's something which is part of each of us, even those of us who might not quite know it yet.

Health That Transcends Time

Now, let's talk science, but let's keep it real. The health benefits of running extend far beyond the physical; they ripple through our mental and emotional well-being as well. Regular running strengthens the heart, boosts lung power, regulates blood sugar levels, and helps manage body weight. Yet, what's often left unsaid is that running helps you feel vibrantly alive. More alert. More grounded. More authentically you. From a personal perspective, those times in my life when I have been able to run consistently have without doubt resulted in me being a more balanced, happier individual with a better sense of personal value and higher self-esteem. All positive attributes in improving my mental health. Not only am I more confident, I sleep better, I have clearer thought processes, my skin is clearer and for all intents and purposes I am on the whole an improved version of my non-running self. I feel closer to the real me.

That said, you certainly don't have to take my word for it. Numerous studies have illuminated the profound connection between running and mental health, linking regular physical activity to reduced rates of anxiety, depression, and cognitive decline. When you run, your body releases a cascade of chemicals, endorphins, dopamine, and serotonin. All of which significantly help to enhance your mood and cognitive function, transforming your mental landscape. You not only feel good; you think clearer and handle life's challenges with greater ease.

The benefits of running often extend to life's more challenging moments. When you're navigating grief, burnout (and believe me I can share a story or two about burnout) or heartbreak, it's frequently the rhythm of your footsteps that brings you back to center. That steady beat of movement becomes a conversation with your own resilience, a reassuring reminder that you have the strength to endure and adapt. Each run is a reaffirmation of your body's capabilities and a testament to your mind's ability to rise above adversity.

Moreover, running contributes significantly to better sleep quality. Quality sleep is paramount for cognitive function, emotional stability, and overall health. The physical exertion of running helps to regulate your circadian rhythms, allowing for deeper, more restorative sleep cycles. When you wake up refreshed, you're not only ready to tackle the day at hand but also armed with improved clarity of thought and emotional balance.

Running as Rebellion

In contemporary society, we inhabit a world designed for sitting, for swiping, and for scrolling through curated lives on screens. This digital age can sometimes feel devoid of genuine connection and fulfillment. I am sure that we have all lost more time than we care to admit to the dreaded and never-ending process of doom scrolling on our phones or tablets. I the face of this digital world running stands as an act of rebellion against this paradigm. A bold declaration that you choose to reclaim your autonomy. When you run, you declare: "I choose effort over ease. I choose presence over autopilot. I choose to move forward: both literally and metaphorically."

Engaging in running teaches us invaluable lessons about discomfort and resilience. Each time you lace up your shoes and push through the initial reluctance, you learn to lean into discomfort and embrace the process. You figure out how to keep going, especially when fatigue sets in, and the urge to stop is overwhelming. It's a powerful metaphor for life: often, the most meaningful growth occurs in moments of challenge and resistance.

Running becomes a vehicle for self-discovery, your path marked by sweat and grit. You realize that those feelings of tiredness or doubt are just part of the journey, not roadblocks to your progress. By consistently choosing to run, you reinforce the understanding that perseverance is essential, both on the track and in everyday life. Some people call this never giving up.

The Nature Connection

Engaging with nature transforms the experience of running from a simple exercise into a profound connection with the world around us. When you step outside and run through a forest trail, along a beach at low tide, or a park bathed in the warm glow of sunrise, something ancient within you awakens.

Nature has a unique ability to ground us, pulling our focus away from the chaos of daily life and into the present moment. You breathe in the world around you, feel the varied terrain beneath your feet, and start to notice things far beyond the confines of your smartphone screen. The gentle rustle of leaves, the distant sound of waves, the changing colors of the sky, all of these become part of your running experience and by extension a bigger part of your overcall life experience.

This deep connection transcends the physical act of running; it is a means of engaging with the environment, reminding us of our place within the natural world. Running in nature heightens our awareness, calling forth a sense of awe and wonder for the beauty that surrounds us. Each run becomes a silent dialogue with the earth, a moving meditation, a living prayer that nourishes not just the body but the spirit. Leaving with it an unwritten agreement between your mind and nature that you will see each other again next time.

Even when you find yourself on the pavement of a bustling city, the rhythm of your feet tapping the ground can still serve as a means of reconnecting with yourself and your environment. The simple act of running allows you to carve out a refuge within, helping to ground you amidst the whirlwind of life. In these situations, I try to be thankful, not only that I am able to be out running, but also that I have been able to decide to do it. I remind myself that I run both because I can and because I choose to, not because I have to. Even on my slowest runs and the days when fitness is but a murmur in the distance, I imagine that I will inspire one person who walks past me, one person who looks out of their window. I imagine the discussion in their head saying, look at the state of that, if he can do then so can I. That nourishes my soul and positively feeds my mental health needs.

The Spirit in Stride

For many, running evolves into a spiritual practice—not because they set out to create one, but because it quietly becomes that. There's something transcendent about placing one foot in front of the other, repeatedly, until the noise of the world falls away, leaving only breath and motion.

In moments of solitude and stillness, profound revelations often surface. Feelings once buried under the weight of daily life emerge. Ideas flow in a way they never do while sitting still. It's here, in this tranquil space created by movement, that peace often finds its way into our hearts. Running strips away the distractions, delivering us to the raw essence of being alive.

You don't need a temple or incense to experience this; all you need is a pair of shoes and an open heart. Each run becomes an opportunity to listen to your inner voice, to reflect on your journey, and to cultivate a sense of gratitude for your body and its capabilities.

We Run Together

Even in solitude, running carries a communal heartbeat. Throughout history, from Indigenous tribes who ran to carry messages between villages to today's weekend running clubs and massive race events, running has the power to create connection, camaraderie, and a shared language spoken through breath and grit.

You might start running with the intention of being alone, but often, you will find your people along the way. You will discover that this is about the journey more than it will ever be about the destination. You will inevitably find yourself surrounded by others who share your dedication to movement and growth, you forge bonds beyond mere acquaintances. It's here, amidst fellow runners, that you often find your tribe, those people who encourage, uplift, and understand the journey you're on.

Running transcends status, profession, and social barriers. It creates a unique space where we care less about our day-to-day stress and more about the simple shared experience of moving forward together. The moments spent shoulder to shoulder at mile seven, laughing and struggling, become a testament to the human spirit.

Ultimately, is that not what we all desire? To be seen, supported and encouraged. To be carried forward, by community, to be part of something and to belong.

A Return, Not a Beginning

So, whether you're just getting started or returning to the sport after a hiatus, it's vital to understand you are not starting from scratch. You're diving back into something deep and powerful, something that has always been a part of you.

Running is not about how fast you go or who finishes first. It's about the journey toward discovering more of yourself.

It's about movement and meaning and everything in between that will ultimately lead you to better balance.

Your Call to Action: Begin the Journey

Before you proceed to the next chapter, take a moment to pause and reflect. Inhale deeply, and let your thoughts settle.

Ask yourself:

- What do I want to discover on this journey?
- What have I been running from, or toward?
- What would it mean for me to run with my heart?

Now, take one simple action: lace up your shoes. Step outside. Walk if you need to, run if you can. But begin. because the moment you do, you're not just running, you're remembering who you are and this is the act of granting yourself permission to explore this wonderous journey, that will bring you closer to discovering yourself than you thought possible.

FINDING YOUR
RHYTHM

PACE

CADENCE

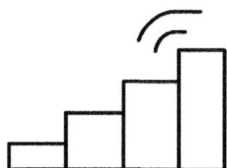

IMPORTANCE OF
CONSISTENCY

FEBRUARY

Chapter 2:
FEBRUARY

Finding rhythm, understanding pace, cadence and the importance of consistency.

Seasonal Reflection:

February often brings unpredictable weather, echoing the ups and downs of life. Ice and rain can make running a challenge, yet this is a great opportunity to remind ourselves that each step taken in adversity builds resilience.

Mindfulness Theme:

Utilize the difficulty of running in adverse conditions to practice acceptance. Cultivate a mindset that embraces challenges and learns to find joy even in discomfort.

Mental Health Insight:

Recognize the importance of setting small, achievable goals during this month to combat feelings of inadequacy. Each completed run, no matter how difficult, reinforces a sense of accomplishment.

February Mantra:

"I find my rhythm, I trust the flow, I grow with every step."

Finding Your Rhythm

As the days of February unfold, the world outside begins to wake from its winter slumber. The air is still crisp, with playful hints of warmth gently encouraging us to shed our layers and emerge from hibernation. Just as nature finds its rhythm in this transition, heralded by the gradual lengthening of days, so too are we invited to discover our unique cadence and pace along the journey of running.

Historically, humans have always been attuned to the rhythm of nature, from the cyclical patterns of lunar phases to the migration of animals and the blooming of flowers. Ancient cultures celebrated these rhythms through rituals, songs, and dances that resonated with the natural world around them. Early agricultural societies, for instance, synchronized their planting and harvesting with the changing seasons, understanding that their survival depended on their ability to flow with nature's tempo. In much the same way, each runner must learn to listen to the heartbeat of their own journey, a process that requires patience, exploration, and a willingness to embrace the ebb and flow of personal growth. February is a perfect time to remind ourselves that progress is not linear, much like the month itself where you can experience every type of weather known to human kind.

Finding your rhythm is not merely about hitting the ground in a steady beat. It's a meditative practice, harmonizing the mind and body as they move in sync with the environment around you. This chapter will guide you into the heart of pacing and rhythm and illuminate how these elements can elevate your experience while highlighting the importance of consistency and our connection to the natural world.

The Dance of Pace and Cadence

Pace and cadence are the heartbeats of your running journey, driving forces that bring harmony to your movement. But what do these terms mean, and how can they enhance your experience?

Pace is often measured in minutes per mile or kilometers; it's your speed, a tempo that dictates how you feel throughout your run. Reflect on how a piece of music stretches and pulls at its tempo. Too fast, and it can feel overwhelming, much like racing against your capabilities. This frenetic pace can lead to burnout and frustration, pulling you away from the joy that running can bring. Conversely, a comfortably sustainable pace invites enjoyment and transformation, turning each run into an exploration rather than a race against time. Remember to be kind to yourself, allow yourself more time to experience the journey and to connect with both you and the environment.

Cadence, on the other hand, refers to the number of steps you take per minute—the rhythm that provides the foundation for your movement. Picture your body as a finely tuned instrument; a higher cadence indicates a lighter, more fluid sound, while a lower cadence might resemble the heavier clunk of an untuned piano. Studies suggest that a cadence of approximately 170-180 steps per minute can enhance running efficiency and minimize the risk of injury, allowing you to glide through your run with ease.

While the science behind these metrics is useful, it's vital to discover what works best for you personally. Every runner possesses a unique rhythm shaped by variables like body mechanics, experience, and personal preference. By tuning into your body and listening to its signals, you can gradually experiment with different paces and cadences. Challenge yourself to find that sweet spot where you feel strong, light, and free.

Harmonizing Mind and Body

When you run, you unite your physical self with your mental resolve, a synergy that fosters growth on both fronts. Channeling your mental focus allows you to shy away from distractions and truly embrace the experience of running. Through consistent practice, you nurture a state of mindfulness, helping you connect the rhythm of your breath with the tempo of your steps.

But this connection is not merely one-sided. As the rhythm of your body aligns with the pulse of the earth, you tap into a deeper consciousness. Being outdoors amplifies this experience; with each step, your feet contact the ground, and your body absorbs the energy of nature in motion. On a good day you will feel alive, the world re-energizing you more than any carbon plated shoe could ever hope to.

Imagine the simple act of running through a forest: the rustling leaves and chirping birds create a symphony supporting the adventure unfolding within you. Notice how the sunlight filters through the trees, casting playful shadows on the path. These moments don't just pass by; they become part of your running narrative, weaving a richer tapestry of experience. With each inhalation, you draw in the crisp, invigorating air; with every exhalation, you release the tensions of everyday life. Not only do you become more relaxed and smoother, but your fluidity will improve as you subconsciously synchronize ever more closely with the world which shares every run with you.

Nature's Influence on Our Consistency

As you build your established routine, let the essence of nature guide you toward consistency. Take a lesson from the world around you: observe how the seasons interact, transform, and persist. Growth is rarely straight-lined; it ebbs and flows, guided by external conditions. Just as spring does not rush toward summer but unfolds gracefully, we too must pace ourselves through our running journey.

Consider creating a running schedule that works harmoniously with nature. Embrace February's distinct beauty as a time for reflection and renewal. Set aside specific days to engage with the elements, rambling over new trails, taking note of the shifting landscape, or stopping to appreciate nature's artistry in winter's fleeting glory. Allow your runs to become experiences that transcend physical exercise, morphing into meditation in motion.

Consistency in running, much like a healthy ecosystem, thrives through nurturing habits. There will be days filled with motivation, where the skies are blue, and your legs feel like they could carry you for miles. But there will also be gray days when motivation wanes, and your body may protest. These challenges are part of the journey, like the storms that occasionally sweep across the changing seasons.

However, like nature's resilience, your ability to show up, regardless of circumstances, creates the groundwork for transformation. Studies show that habitual runners report lower stress and increased mental clarity, tying physical activity directly to heightened resilience during life's ups and downs. Make a commitment to honor your routine even on the less glamorous days, reaping the rewards of dedication over time.

Understand the Rhythm of Your Journey

Finding your rhythm is deeply personal and can often mirror the natural world around you. Like a river's meander, once again take this opportunity to remind yourself that your journey will not always be linear; some days may flow effortlessly while others might feel like you're trudging through mud. Embrace both experiences as vital threads in the fabric of your story, for they reveal growth and understanding.

Running is about exploration, not only of your surroundings but also your limits and capabilities. Cherish moments when you float through your stride, when pace and cadence intertwine seamlessly. Let that exhilarating feeling wash over you, reminding you why you lace up your shoes: for the freedom, the joy, and the exhilarating dance of movement that connects you to nature.

Finding Flow in February

As February opens doors to new beginnings, leverage this fertile ground for cultivating your rhythm. Set intentions that honor your unique path and reflect the lessons learned in this chapter. Perhaps you aim to refine your pace or discover the cadence that aligns with your flow.

Take inspiration from early bloomers of spring that break through the frost, reminding you that growth can be deliberate and gradual yet profoundly transformative. In a season where the world around you is shifting, allow yourself the grace to navigate your journey while celebrating your unique path.

Invite nature's embrace into your runs. Consider finding a favorite route that showcases the beauty of this transitional month; watch trees crackle and pop as they return to life or listen to the unmistakable call of birds re-establishing their nests. Allow these experiences to anchor you in each run, refreshing both body and spirit.

Your Call to Action: Tune into Your Rhythm

As you embark on this month of finding your rhythm, take a moment to set intentions that empower you on this journey. Here are some guiding questions to help shape your experience:

- What is your ideal pace, and how does it feel as you move at that speed? Take note of how your body responds to various paces and adjust accordingly.
- In what ways can you cultivate consistency in your running practice? Reflect on how you can integrate your running routine with the rhythms of nature.

- How does nature inspire your runs, and what do you notice during your time outdoors?

Make a conscious effort to observe the environment, allowing it to invigorate your experience. a specific action for your runs this February. Set a goal around practicing a particular rhythm, increasing your cadence, or deepening your connection to nature during your runs. Make sure it resonates with your spirit and propels you forward on this beautiful journey.

Before you venture outside, take a moment to acknowledge the world around you: the fragrant earth beneath your feet, the gentle whispers of the trees, and the refreshing kiss of the air. Allow these elements to amplify your experience as you navigate your path.

Now, head out the door: lace up your shoes, find a route that excites you, and immerse yourself in the rhythm of each step. Pay attention to your pace, savor every moment, and let your body explore the beautiful symphony it feels most alive in. Because the true power lies not just in the act of running but in uncovering the dance that is uniquely yours.

You are in the flow, and that, above all, is where the magic happens.

FROM MINDSET
TO MILES

MINDSET   MENTAL   MILES
TOUGHNESS

MARCH

Chapter 3:
MARCH

From mindset to miles. Developing a runners mindset and mental toughness.

Seasonal Reflection:

As spring begins to stir, nature starts to bloom. The thaw of winter brings vibrant colors and fresh energy, paralleling your own renewal in mindset and body.

Mindfulness Theme:

Acknowledge the beauty of transformation during your runs. Pay attention to the sights and sounds around you; the sounds of birds singing, or the scent of fresh earth can serve as gentle reminders of your own growth.

Mental Health Insight:

This month encourages a shift in perspective. Running among fresh blooms can lift your mood and inspire gratitude, reinforcing the connection between nature and mental well-being.

March Mantra:

"Breathe in courage. Breathe out doubt."

From Mindset to Miles

As we welcome March, the promise of spring hangs in the air and even if you can't see it, you can certainly sense it. An electrifying whisper of renewal for the earth and our running journeys. With winter's grip beginning to loosen, you can almost hear the world waking up, shedding its heavy blanket of frost, and preparing to burst forth in vibrant colors. Just as the landscape around us undergoes a transformation, so too can your running journey evolve through the development of mental toughness. Across the following pages, we will delve more deeply into the complexities of mindset and resilience, exploring how these traits have been woven into the very fabric of our human history and more importantly how they can empower your running and life today.

The Historical Roots of Running

Remember, long before organized sports or weekend fun runs existed, running was an essential skill for early humans, an instinctual expression of survival. Imagine our ancestors, finely tuned for endurance, moving across vast landscapes with remarkable agility and grace. They relied on running to hunt, gather, and protect themselves from the perils of a wild and unpredictable world. Researchers have found that early humans' physical traits—straight backs, powerful legs, and an efficient cooling system through sweating—equipped them perfectly for the long-distance running they needed to do. Contrast that with an increasing trend in the modern world where people are increasingly house bound, through choice, sitting in front of a desk all day working from home and using any manner of phone apps to have meals or groceries delivered straight to your door.

It is also worth noting that it was not merely physical prowess that allowed our ancestors to thrive; it was mental toughness. The continuation of movement amid exhaustion, fear, and unpredictability. Each mile traversed in pursuit of survival was an exercise in resilience. Just as these early runners drew upon their sheer willpower to overcome the challenges of their environment, you too can tap into that same spirit as you lace up your running shoes today. This is evidence enough that our bodies are capable of so much more than we could ever imagine, but we need to take the time and build a mindset that can support this.

The Power of Positive Thinking

Mental toughness or mental resilience in running begins with learning how to cultivate positive thinking, a vital component that can make all the difference in your performance. Durable optimism acts like a shield, fortifying you against self-doubt and external stressors. Practice reworking your internal dialogue, just as our ancestors would have needed to maintain a hopeful mindset in the face of adversity.

Consider this: your body is a temple built for endurance, capable of remarkable feats. Facing those inevitable challenges, remind yourself of your strength: "I can conquer this mile." Acknowledge the power of intention in shaping your mindset and running experience. Say it out loud and make it real to and for you. Embrace your thoughts and commit to your words, when it gets tough remind yourself that you "can conquer the next step", we don't build a house all at the same time, we put it together brick by brick.

Building positive routines can be powerful in your journey and daily affirmations can impart an immense boost to your self-belief. After you get out of bed each morning, stand tall in front of a mirror, look yourself in the eyes, and declare your worth: "I am strong. I am capable. I can overcome obstacles." Make this ritual part of your daily routine. Such simple actions can lead to profound shifts in mindset, just as rituals around fire and community may have served early humans in solidifying their bonds and encouraging shared successes.

Nature as a Teacher

As you run, continue to pay special attention to the world around you. With March beckoning the start of spring, nature is an extraordinary teacher of resilience and adaptability. The plants and animals have weathered the harshness of winter, and now they respond to the longer days and warmer temperatures with remarkable vigor. Witnessing this rebirth can inspire your running journey. I know that this inspires me, not only in my runs but more profoundly. This is a reminder that we are all part of something more and as the plants and animals go through this visible re-birth it helps me to check in with myself and plays a part in re-validating my sense of purpose. I am not everything, I am part of something much bigger, and how exciting is that!

Let's take the example of trees. They bend and sway with the wind, demonstrating flexibility while remaining deeply rooted. Just as trees adapt to their environment, weathering storms, stretching toward the sun, you too can learn to bend rather than break when faced with challenges on your runs. Listen to the whispers of nature; they resonate with the spirit of resilience that lives within you.

Embracing Discomfort:
A Path to Mental Toughness

To cultivate mental toughness, you must also learn to embrace discomfort. Every runner, regardless of experience, encounters physical fatigue, pain, and moments of self-doubt. The act of running often brings forth the rawness of our human experience each heartbeat, each breath, each struggle mirrors those early days of humanity when survival was paramount.

When you face discomfort during your runs, take a moment to embrace it. Instead of dreading the burn in your muscles or the ache in your joints, reframe it as a sign of growth, a confirmation that you are challenging yourself and evolving. Imagine your ancestor's outpacing danger while their muscles screamed for reprieve. They did not allow discomfort to dominate their journey; rather, they pushed through, relying on their inherent resilience. They believed in themselves, even if only out of necessity, they accepted the pain, and this allowed them to be fully committed to the next step.

To enhance your comfort with discomfort, incorporate specific workouts designed to challenge you. Consider hill sprints, tempo runs, and even long-distance runs that extend beyond your current capability. The carefully calculated stress of these workouts mimics the varied challenges of early life and allows your body and mind to adapt. After all, growth occurs outside of your comfort zone.

Mindfulness in Motion

As you begin to embrace discomfort, it becomes essential to cultivate a mindful awareness around your running. Mindfulness can provide a sanctuary, allowing you to observe your thoughts and emotions without judgment. Ground yourself in the present moment, tuning into the sensations of your body and the environment around you.

Practice running without distractions, leave the music behind and instead listen to the rhythm of your breath and the sounds of nature. Be aware of the wind brushing against your skin, the temperature of the sun on your back, or the earthy scent of damp soil beneath your feet. This engagement with the present moment allows you to build resilience, transforming your runs into meditative experiences.

As our ancestors navigated their environments, they relied on their senses to assess potential threats or opportunities. With your senses engaged, you foster a deep connection with nature, reminding yourself of your own roots and the lineage of runners who came before you.

Visualization: Seeing Your Success

Visualization is an extraordinary technique that has stood the test of time and is crucial in building a runner's mindset. Just as early humans honed their skills through shared experiences, you can mentally play out your runs before they even happen, crafting mental images that reinforce your determination and goals.

Find a quiet space: perhaps a peaceful meadow, a calm forest glade, or your favorite spot at home. Close your eyes and envision your upcoming runs in vivid detail: the route you will take, the rhythm of your feet hitting the ground, and the sense of accomplishment you'll feel as you cross that finish line, whether it's the one for a race or simply your goal for the day.

Try to incorporate the emotions that accompany your visualization. Feel the pride, the joy, the sense of achievement. The more intricate and emotionally charged your visualizations are, the more powerful they become. Allow these mental images to fuel your motivation during training and empower you to notice the strength of your resolve.

Setting Intentions and Goals

With spring on the horizon, March provides a perfect opportunity to reflect on your running journey and establish intentional goals. Engaging in this process helps solidify your focus and a sense of direction, paving the way for success.

Take time to set SMART goals: Specific, Measurable, Achievable, Relevant, and Time-bound. A well-defined goal fuels purpose and helps you channel your training effectively. Maybe you wish to conquer a certain distance, set a personal record, or explore new trails, whatever your objectives may be, grounding them in these parameters increases your chances of fulfillment.

Once your goals are set, write them down and make them visible. Place them somewhere you will see them daily, such as on your bathroom mirror or next to your running gear, where they serve as motivators to keep you accountable. Reflect on them regularly. The act of acknowledging your progress, as this mirrors what our ancestors did as they shared their triumphs and stories within their communities.

Celebrate Milestones: Create mini milestones along your journey and integrate celebration into the process. Whether short distances completed, or personal bests achieved, each step forward in your journey deserves recognition. This sharing forms connections that validate your efforts and foster a sense of belonging, echoing the communal spirit that defined early human societies.

Building a Supportive Running Community

As you forge ahead in your running journey, a supportive community can play a pivotal role in nurturing a strong runner's mindset. Surrounding yourself with like-minded individuals enhances motivation and fosters accountability. You can find encouragement in moments of struggle and joy during times of success.

Engage with local running groups, participate in social media platforms, or organize meetups with friends who share your passion. These connections can provide a wealth of experience and camaraderie, amplifying your commitment to those goals that you have committed to.

Think back to our ancestors gathering around flames, relaying tales of their victories and hardships. They thrived in community, drawing strength from one another. Similarly, share your progress and challenges openly with your fellow runners. Each shared story weaves the fabric of support and understanding, creating a network of encouragement.

You might form a running buddy system for enhanced accountability. Find someone to tackle your goals with, whether through a regular running schedule, spontaneous jogs, or workout check-in over coffee. As you lift each other up, you create a circle of influence that reinforces both your journeys.

Your Call to Action: Strengthen Your Mindset

As you dive into March and make strides toward your running goals, now is the time to focus on building your runner's mindset. Here are practical steps to help you harness the power of resilience and determination:

1. Practice Daily Affirmations: Develop a list of affirmations that inspire you. Commit to reciting them each morning, letting the affirmative energy carry you through the day.

2. Embrace Discomfort: Challenge yourself weekly. Integrate one workout that pushes

your limits, then reflect on how confronting discomfort strengthens your resolve.

3. Visualize Your Success: Set aside a moment each week for visualization. Picture your runs, feel the emotion of achievement, and embody the runner you want to become.

4. Set SMART Goals: Define at least one specific, measurable goal for March that resonates with your journey. Keep track of your progress and adjust as needed. Remember these goals need to be specific, measurable, achievable, realistic and time bound.

5. Engage with Your Community: Reach out to fellow runners. Share your experiences and celebrate milestones collectively, allow that shared energy to fuel your passion. If you don't know where to begin, start by connecting with me on Strava, where you will find me under the name RonnieC.

As you lace up your shoes and embrace the vibrancy of spring, remember that running is more than mere miles; it's about the journey of cultivating resilience that transcends the act of exercise. Draw strength from nature and the ancestors who paved the way, allow their spirit to echo within you as you run. Visualize this when the hard yards hit, picture your ancestors their shoulder to shoulder right beside you, accept any pain that you might be feeling and grant yourself permission to take the next step, and then the next one, and then the next one.

You possess the power to shape your running experience and your life. Do not hesitate to take that first step today, blending the ancient wisdom of endurance with today's determination and revel in the miles ahead, buoyed by courage and tenacity.

FUELING YOUR
PASSION

NUTRITION   HYDRATION   IMPORTANCE

APRIL

Chapter 4:
APRIL

Fueling your passion. Nutrition, hydration and the importance of fueling your runs.

Seasonal Reflection:

April showers bring May flowers, reminding us that growth often requires enduring challenges. The rain can feel refreshing and invigorating during your runs. It is important to remember that the work you put in today, will reap rewards tomorrow.

Mindfulness Theme:

Approach each run as a form of playful exploration. The rhythmic sound of raindrops can become a meditative soundtrack, encouraging you to let go and be present in the moment.

Mental Health Insight:

The act of running outside can remind you of life's simple joys, increasing feelings of happiness and connectedness. Journal about your experiences after runs to deepen your reflections.

April Mantra:

"Fuel strong. Run steady. Burn bright."

Fueling Your Passion

As April unfolds, the world around us bursts forth in a riot of colors and life. Trees blossom with delicate flowers, fields awaken with vibrant greens, and the air carries the sweet scent of renewal. Just as spring nurtures nature's revival, this month invites us to rejuvenate our bodies through thoughtful nutrition and hydration. Essential components of any runner's journey, the right fuel not only supports performance but also deepens your connection with the environment and your own inner vitality.

A Historical Perspective on Fueling the Body

Whilst the relationship between diet and athletic performance is as old as humanity itself. The link between effective fueling and mental health is not only often overlooked but also regularly misunderstood. From ancient civilizations to modern athletes, the understanding of how nutrition impacts endurance and resilience has continually evolved. Early runners, much like today's athletes, were aware of the power of food as fuel. Their diets were often dictated by their surroundings, predominantly consisting of whole foods sourced from nature, including fruits, vegetables, grains, and proteins.

Historically, the ancient Greeks celebrated the nutritional benefits of food within their athletic culture, honoring the connection between sustenance and performance. In the time of the Olympics, athletes were encouraged to consume a diet rich in barley, figs, honey, and wine. These foods provided the energy needed for their physically demanding rites and competitions.

The native peoples of the Americas used local resources to fuel their endurance. The running tribes revered their connection with the earth, often consuming unique energy-boosting foods such as chia seeds. The ancient Tarahumara, known for their incredible long-distance running capabilities, relied on a diet featuring natural staples like corn and beans, supplemented by homemade energy gels made from chia seeds and honey, drawing energy directly from the earth around them and further strengthens the link between fuel, endurance and resilience.

Understanding this historical context enhances our appreciation of nutritional wisdom passed down through generations. As runners today, we stand on the shoulders of those who paved the way for us, harnessing the knowledge of what it means to truly fuel our passion.

Nutrition: The Building Blocks of Endurance

Nutrition is not merely about consumption; it's a nuanced dance between choice, balance, and the art of listening to your body. The journey of a runner requires fuel, both in the form of macronutrients and micronutrients, to support training, recovery, and overall well-being.

Macronutrients are the three primary components of our diet: carbohydrates, proteins, and fats—all of which play significant roles in fueling performance.

Carbohydrates are often heralded as the essential fuel for runners, carbohydrates provide the quick energy required for your workouts. Foods such as whole grains, fruits, and vegetables are rich sources, sustaining your energy levels both during training and throughout the day. As you run, your body primarily relies on carbohydrates stored as glycogen in your muscles and liver.

Proteins: these nutrients are the building blocks of muscles and are particularly crucial for recovery. After exertion, your body craves protein to repair and strengthen muscle tissue. Incorporating lean meats, legumes, dairy, and nuts into your diet helps facilitate this recovery.

Fats, while often misunderstood, healthy fats are a vital energy source, especially for longer runs. Foods like avocados, olive oil, and nuts not only provide sustained energy but also support overall heart health and hormone synthesis.

A balanced diet rich in these macronutrients ensures that your body receives the necessary resources to optimize performance and recovery.

Micronutrients, vitamins and minerals may not provide energy directly, but they are essential for maintaining optimal bodily functions, ranging from immune support to energy production. Iron, calcium, magnesium, and B vitamins, for instance, contribute significantly to stamina and endurance.

Fueling your body with a rainbow of fruits and vegetables not only supports your physical health but also draws you closer to the vibrant world around you. Seasonal produce offers an array of vitamins while grounding you in the present moment. As you savor the flavors of springtime produce, embrace that connection with nature, letting each bite be a deliberate choice fueled by gratitude.

The Art of Hydration

In addition to nutrition, hydration serves as a cornerstone for performance, especially as the temperatures begin to rise in April. Our bodies are composed primarily of water, and staying properly hydrated is crucial for maintaining optimal bodily functions. Hydration impacts endurance, power output, and the body's ability to efficiently regulate temperature.

Understanding the importance of hydration goes beyond a mere sip of water before a run; it's about cultivating habits that prioritize fluid intake throughout the day. As early as the Greeks, hydration was recognized as fundamental athletes often consumed large quantities of water before competition to ensure peak performance.

Listen to your body! Simple cues like thirst can guide you, but proactive hydration habits are essential. Carry a water bottle during your day-to-day activities and set reminders on your phone if needed.

Timing is another essential aspect of hydration. A good rule of thumb recommends drinking water consistently throughout the day, not just during or after exercise. Aim for approximately 16 to 20 ounces (500-600 ml) of water two hours before your run. During your workout, strive to drink 7 to 10 ounces (200-300 ml) every 10 to 20 minutes. Post-run, aim to replenish what you lost through sweat and exertion, aiming to drink at least 24 ounces (700 ml) of water for every pound (0.45 kg) lost during the run.

Natural sources of hydration come in various forms, from fresh fruits and vegetables to herbal teas. Melons, cucumbers, and oranges are especially hydrating choices that double as nutrition. Additionally, infusing water with slices of citrus or herbs can transform hydration into a revitalizing experience that aligns with the season of renewal.

Honoring the Rhythms of Nature

April is a time of rebirth not just for nature but for our running routines. As the days lengthen and the weather grows warmer, allow this season to inspire your relationship with food and hydration. Embrace the bounty of seasonal fruits and vegetables, rejoicing in fresh, nourishing ingredients.

Spend time at a local farmer's market, where communities connect over fresh produce. Purchase seasonal berries, asparagus, artichokes, or spring peas, cultivating a deeper connection with the cycle of nature. Take a moment to appreciate the origins of these foods and the labor of those who grow them. Not only will your body reap the benefits of nutritious foods, but your soul may find fulfillment in fostering a community-centered relationship with food.

This connection to the earth can amplify your enjoyment of running. Picture how our ancestors may have approached running—flourishing in unison with their surroundings, drawing energy and sustenance directly from the land. Reflect on their journeys as mushrooms grow in the unfurling warmth, or how wildflowers burst forth from patches of earth, using their roots to draw water and nutrients.

The Importance of Fueling Before and After Runs

As you cultivate a supportive nutrition and hydration routine, consider how food choices can significantly influence your running experience. Anticipating your fueling needs before hitting the pavement can make a monumental difference.

Pre-run Fuel. Just as racehorses are examined and prepped before a crucial race, preparing your body for a run requires thoughtful attention to nutrition. Consuming a balanced meal rich in carbohydrates an hour or two before your workout ensures that your body has accessible energy. Options such as oatmeal topped with fruit or a banana with nut butter provide the essential fuel for sustained energy.

Consider creating your own energy bars using natural ingredients like dates, oats, and nuts for a quick, nutritious pre-run snack. Not only can these bars be customized to meet your palate, but they also affirm your creativity and connection to the earth from which they are derived.

Post-run Recovery: Post-workout nutrition is equally crucial. After pushing your body to its limits, it craves replenishment. Aim to eat a combination of carbohydrates and protein within 30-60 minutes of finishing your run to facilitate muscle repair. A simple smoothie or yogurt topped with fruit helps refuel glycogen stores while providing the necessary protein for recovery.

Recognize that this ritual of nurturing your body after runs echoes the practices of ancient athletes. They prioritized recovery, understanding its significance in readiness for their next challenge. Allow that knowledge to integrate into your habits as you savor each post-run snack.

Listening to Your Body's Signals

As you implement nutrition and hydration strategies into your routine, perhaps the most invaluable lesson is the importance of listening to your body. Our innate wisdom often indicates what it needs, whether that be nourishment, hydration, rest, or recovery.

Learn to attune yourself to hunger cues, distinguishing between physiological and emotional hunger. As you become more mindful of your eating habits, you may find that you crave specific nutrients your body needs at any given time. Engaging with whole foods fosters a connection to both your physical health and your intuition.

Reflect on your hydration habits. Are you properly hydrating before, during, and after your runs? Implement small changes to your daily routine, like adding a glass of water with every meal or decanting water into a more visually appealing vessel to make hydration feel special.

Establishing Healthy Rituals

As with all forms of self-care, establishing nurturing rituals surrounding nutrition and hydration can enhance your overall well-being. Consider how rituals resonate within the fabric of our lives—from meal preparation infused with intention to practices that ground us in connection with our environment.

Create a weekly ritual dedicated to meal planning. Spend time preparing family-style meals filled with wholesome ingredients that you can share with loved ones. Engage others in conversation or assign tasks, turning cooking into a communal experience that celebrates nourishment and togetherness.

Explore seasonal recipes that highlight local produce. For example, delight in a spring salad bursting with arugula, fresh strawberries, and nuts drizzled with balsamic vinaigrette. By incorporating nature's colors and flavors into your meals, you foster a sense of unity and connection with the changing world around you.
With every bite and sip, you reaffirm your commitment to fueling your passion, acknowledging that nurturing your body contributes to an overall sense of vitality. Allow these rituals to resonate as

you form bonds with others who share a commitment to health and wellness.

Your Call to Action: Embrace the Power of Nutrition and Hydration

As April blossoms into full swing, draw upon the knowledge and inspiration to fuel your passion effectively. Here are some practical steps to enhance your approach to nutrition and hydration:

1. Assess Your Current Nutrition: For one week, take note of what you consume daily. Reflect on the balance of macronutrients and the colors of fruits and vegetables on your plate. Identify areas for improvement. I would recommend simply journaling this rather than using an app, there is something pure about the act of writing and it almost helps you to connect more with the words than if you are simply pressing another button on another app on your tablet or phone.

2. Create a Balanced Meal Plan: Dedicate time this week to prepare a nutrient-dense meal plan. Focus on seasonal foods and incorporate macronutrient-rich meals to support your running.

3. Hydration Cues: Monitor your hydration habits. Set a goal to drink a specific amount

of water daily, using visual reminders or apps to help you stay on track.

4. Experiment with Pre- and Post-Run Snacks: Test different snacks before and after your runs, paying attention to how each choice affects your performance and recovery. Keep a journal to track your findings.

5. Establish a Weekend Meal Prep Ritual: Devote time each weekend to meal prep. Engaging family or friends can make it a joyous occasion, foster connections, and create delicious nourishment.

It will always be the choices that we make that will help us to connect our mind with our physical self. Making better choices more consistently will help us to connect our mind with the miles. Decide what kind of person that you want to be where nutrition is concerned, use food as a net additive to your personal story and to your running journey. Take time to educate yourself and allow yourself the chance to experiment, give yourself permission to make mistakes to find out what works for you on a personal level.

As you lace up your shoes heading into April, remember that the journey of a runner extends beyond the miles ahead; it encompasses the choices we make to fuel our bodies and nurture our spirits. Just as nature flourishes in the embrace of spring, so too can you thrive by honoring the essential relationship between food, hydration, and every step of your running journey.

In a world that thrives on connection to us, to the land, and to one another and allow this season of renewal to inspire your commitment to nurturing both body and soul. With each mindful meal, every sip of water, and every run, let passion flow through you like the very lifeblood of the earth, fueling your pursuit of vitality.

THE POWER OF
COMMUNITY

CONNECTIONS   RUNNERS   LOCAL GROUPS

MAY

Chapter 5:

MAY

The power of community, building connections with fellow runners and joining local running groups.

Seasonal Reflection:

May is often associated with community events and gatherings, as warmer weather brings people together. This is the perfect time for running groups or community races. Use May as a catalyst to embrace all types of community to aid your running journey and be sure to give back as well as to take.

Mindfulness Theme:

Engage with fellow runners and notice the shared energy and support. Mindfulness can stem from these connections as you practice being present in group settings. Take an interest in the journey of others, exploring different types of runners or running groups and share your journey.

Mental Health Insight:

Building relationships while running helps combat loneliness and fosters a sense of belonging. Reflect on how these communal experiences enhance your sense of purpose. Make a note of it and then use that to further underpin intention in your running journey.

Being open to new experiences and opportunities will bring a profoundly positive impact to your mental health and further help you to connect the mind with the miles.

May Mantra:

"Together we move, together we rise — every stride, a shared strength."

Connection and Community

As May unfolds, the world is alive with the zeal of spring—a perfect metaphor for the energy created when passionate individuals come together. The air is filled with laughter, the paths often crowded with runners, and the spirit of camaraderie ignites every step taken. This month is a celebration of community, the power that emerges when like-minded souls unite over a shared passion for running. In this chapter, we will explore the myriads of ways community can shape our journey, delving deep into its historical roots, the nourishing connections it fosters, and the uplifting spirit it cultivates. In fact, the motto at my running club which was passed down from a much-loved previous chairman of the club, is that people need people, and never a truer word was spoken.

The Historical Roots of Running Communities

Long before contemporary running clubs or organized marathons existed, the essence of community was embodied in the running traditions of early civilizations. Across the ages, communities have gathered to celebrate the joy of movement, commemorate achievements, and draw strength from each other.

In ancient Greece, running was an integral part of the Olympic Games, a celebration that united city-states in athletic competition. These events were not merely contests of speed; they were cherished opportunities for individuals from disparate backgrounds to come together, share stories, and honor the communal spirit. The energy exchanged during those competitions transcended victory and defeat, creating bonds that fostered mutual respect and admiration.

Similarly, indigenous cultures worldwide have revered running not only as a means of transportation but also as a communal practice, an opportunity for storytelling and connection. Through organized running events, races served as ritualistic gatherings that reinforced the ties between individuals and their communities. The power of running to forge these connections remains as relevant today as it was centuries ago.

The Commitment to Connection

In our fast-paced modern age, the desire for connection can sometimes take a backseat. However, joining a running community rekindles this fundamental human need. Engaging with fellow runners' nurtures friendship while promoting accountability and motivation. Running can often feel like a solitary endeavor, but when we come together, we discover that we are part of something larger than ourselves. I believe that this is one key area where the digital world can significantly help or augment the physical community around you. We are all in a position today, where at our fingertips we can significantly expand the breadth and depth of our community from being local to being truly global. However, I do encourage that these tools, apps, forums and other digital connections are used to augment and add to your physical engagement, not to replace it.

Local running clubs and groups offer myriad opportunities for individuals to unite, whether through group training sessions, fun runs, or charity events, including volunteering. At its core, community serves as a powerful motivator; it reminds us that we are not alone in our goals or struggles. In the face of fatigue or self-doubt, the encouragement of fellow runners can push us beyond our perceived limits.

Building Lifelong Friendships

In the world of running, friendships often flourish in shared experiences. There is something uniquely bonding about the act of sweating together, rallying around a common goal, and supporting one another along every mile. Whether it's training for a race or recovering from an injury, the solace of community prevents isolation and nurtures our resilience.

Think back to your early days as a runner. Perhaps you were nervous at the idea of joining a group, unsure of your pace or ability. Yet, once you took that courageous step, you discovered a sense of belonging that extended beyond the athletic realm. Many runners recount stories of friendships built during those early mornings while logging miles together, recounting tales of life, laughter, and shared victories.

Consider how often you have given and received encouragement on a tough run, shared a smile during a dawn workout, or celebrated achievements together—from the first mile completed to a personal best on race day. These moments accumulate, weaving a rich tapestry of connection between runners that can last a lifetime. These friendships form a support system that transcends our individual journeys, providing motivation through the highs and lows of life. My own lifelong journey with running has seen me leave the sport and come back to it for different periods of time, sometimes months and sometimes a decade. In each occurrence I have been embraced back into the fold by different communities, different running clubs or groups and I have found this nonjudgmental acceptance to have an extremely positive impact on my own mental health. It is this as much as anything that has led me to describe running as my medicine.

The Value of Local Running Groups

Joining a local running group can transform the trajectory of your running journey. Not only do these communities foster accountability, but they also offer invaluable resources, camaraderie, and opportunities for growth, both as a runner and an individual.

1. Accountability: When you commit to a group, you are more likely to stay dedicated to your training schedule. Knowing others are counting on you for a morning run can be the nudge needed to get out of bed, even on chilly mornings. When you are able, make it your duty to be the light in the room, the energy in your group, be a net additive, be prepared to give and the positive energy you receive in return will be astounding to you, it will be way more impactful than any carbon plated shoes ever could be. This connection wit people and environments will strengthen your mental resolve in a positive and impactful way. However, this cannot happen by chance, you need to take the accountability and have clear intention.

2. Support and Resources: Local running groups are often rich in experience. Novice runners can benefit from the collective wisdom of seasoned members who can offer guidance on form, training plans, and injury prevention. Many groups host workshops, inviting experts to share insights and answer questions, enriching your knowledge as your progress continues. Make the choice to attend these

events, embrace these opportunities and celebrate the new people you meet as much as you do the new education that you receive.

3. Shared Events: Running clubs often organize races, fundraisers, and community events, making connections both within and beyond the group. These experiences not only create team spirit but also strengthen bonds that often extend into lifelong friendships. The energy at a charity race or a community event creates memories that resonate within the hearts of participants. For those at the start of your journey start with a parkrun if you are fortunate enough to be based in a country which has these wonderful organized free 5K events and for those not, then start with a walk/run around the park, or join a couch to 5K program. The most important thing to remember here is not how you start your journey, but that you do start your journey. Make the choice, state the intention, lace up your shoes, engage your mind and get going.

4. Celebration of Diversity: Local running groups often reflect the various backgrounds and abilities of their members. This representation adds beauty to the running community, showcasing the strength that comes from different perspectives and

experiences. Building connections with individuals from all walks of life reminds us of the breadth of humanity and reinforces our commitment to inclusivity.

Finding Your Running Community

As you ponder how best to build out, expand or simply explore your running community and eco-system and how best to connect to different running communities, here are practical steps to help you find a group that resonates with you:

1. Research Local Groups: Investigate local running clubs or groups in your area. Look for those that align with your interests—whether that's a casual group focused on social runs, or a more serious club centered on training for races. As you work through this process, I believe that you will be surprised at both the volume and diversity of available groups, and if you find yourself in the unlikely but possible scenario where there are no groups, this could be your opportunity to step up and start one. Even if it is a first steps community running group. Remember to state your intention and make it happen.

2. Attend a Group Run: Most clubs welcome newcomers and often host organized group runs. Attend a session to experience the

atmosphere firsthand. Notice how the energy ebbs and flows as runners come together, each with their unique story and reason for running.

3. Participate In Events: Join community events, charity races, or group challenges. Engaging in these activities offers excellent opportunities to meet fellow runners and form connections based on shared experiences.

4. Engage On social media: Many running communities exist online, offering virtual support and encouragement. Follow local running clubs or participate in online forums, leveraging the experiences of others to enhance your journey.

5. Be Open To New Friendships: Approach your running experience with curiosity and openness. The friendships you build in these spaces can transcend athleticism, leading to personal growth and lifelong connections.

The Role of Support Systems

A robust support system is paramount in your running journey, offering solace during times of struggle and joy during moments of triumph. As you invest in your running community, consider how you can reciprocate that support—embracing your role as an encourager and friend.

1. Celebrate Each Other: Make it a habit to celebrate fellow runners' achievements, whether they're crossing finish lines or achieving personal milestones. Acknowledge every victory, no matter how small. Each shout of encouragement nurtures the community spirit, reinforcing connections.

2. Share Challenges: Learn to become more open about challenges and setbacks fosters vulnerability and deep companionship, showing that you are not alone in your journey. Sharing your experiences allows you to learn from one another and connect on a more profound level.

3. Be the Encouragement You Seek: As you navigate the challenges of training or personal goals, inspire others by being a beacon of positivity. Offer support to newer members and provide valuable insights or simply lend a listening ear. This cycle of encouragement not only enriches your running community; it blossoms into meaningful friendships.

4. Lead by Example: As you grow in your running practice, take the initiative to participate

actively in your community. Whether it's volunteering for a race, organizing a fun run, or facilitating a discussion circle on running topics, your leadership creates opportunities for everyone to benefit from one another.

The Connection with Nature

Nature plays a significant role in shaping the running experience and fostering community. Trails and parks become the stages for bonding moments, where connections form while surrounded by the beauty of the natural world.

Take a moment to reflect on your favorite running routes: are they winding trails under a canopy of trees or sun-drenched roads lined with blooming flowers? These landscapes invite you to experience both the physical and communal aspects of running. Whether you're traversing the rugged paths of a mountain range or running alongside a serene lake, each run offers a unique chance to connect with nature and fellow enthusiasts.

Group outings can enhance this connection. Consider joining fellow runners for a group trail run, navigating connections forged by the shared environment. Nature provides the backdrop for laughter, conversation, and inspiration, heightening your appreciation for both the sport and community.

Embracing Diverse Perspectives

In this month dedicated to community, acknowledge the diversity that strengthens it. Every individual contributing to a running group brings unique insights, experiences, and perspectives. Embrace the beauty of these differences, tapping into the richness they offer.

Consider how age, background, and ability shape not just the running experience but the relationships formed within those communities. Encourage inclusivity, inviting others to join regardless of pace or technique. The power of unity shines bright when community members support each other, irrespective of their starting points.

By valuing diverse perspectives, you cultivate a warm, welcoming atmosphere where every runner feels empowered to express their journey. Incorporate mentorship opportunities within your groups, connecting seasoned runners with newer members who wish to learn and grow.

Your Call to Action: Cultivate Your Community

As May unfolds, take actionable steps to deepen your relationship with your running community. Here are a few strategies to foster connections and inspire growth:

1. Join a Local Running Group: Take the leap and find a running group that resonates with you. Engage in their activities high and low, cultivating friendships built on shared passions.

2. Participate in Community Events: Seek out local events, such as races or charity fun runs, to both support the community and connect with fellow runners.

3. Organize Group Runs: Take the initiative to organize a casual group run in your neighborhood. Leverage social media platforms to invite others—creating an inclusive environment for all.

4. Celebrate Accomplishments: Make it a habit to recognize and celebrate milestones, whether personal or collective. Send shout-outs on social media or through group messages, nurturing the spirit of encouragement.

5. Engage Openly: Share your challenges, insights, and experiences with your running community. Foster connections based on

vulnerability, allowing the group to learn and grow together.

As you lace up your shoes and prepare for the journey ahead, realize that community fabricates the backdrop of your running narrative. Togetherness embodies the spirit of running, fostering bonds that elevate us to new heights. Embrace the power of community as we flow through May—discovering joy in shared experiences, laughter in every mile, and strength in every connection.

Standing on the threshold of personal and communal growth, celebrate the vibrant spirit of camaraderie. Whether alongside a seasoned runner or someone just beginning their journey, allow the warmth of community to fuel your passion as you explore the paths ahead.

EMBRACING THE GREAT OUTDOORS

RUNNING   NATURE   TERRAINS

JUNE

Chapter 6:
JUNE

Embracing the Great Outdoors and exploring the Joys of Running in Nature and different terrains

Seasonal Reflection:

The long days of June invite you to explore new trails and expand your horizons. Your endurance is growing alongside nature's vibrant display.

Mindfulness Theme:

Take time during runs to reflect on your personal growth. Consider how your training parallels nature's abundance—embrace the idea that every mile contributes to your journey.

Mental Health Insight:

Celebrate your progress and accomplishments. Recognize that just as nature thrives in the sun, so too can your spirit flourish when nurtured with positivity and self-love.

June Mantra:

"I run with the wind, rooted in the earth, alive in every step."

Embracing the Great Outdoors

As June arrives, the world becomes more vibrant and alive, bursting with the lush greens of trees, the colorful blooms of wildflowers, and the warm embrace of the sun. The allure of the great outdoors beckons every runner to step outside, reveling in the beauty and transformative power of running in nature. This month be sure to explore the many joys of running through varied landscapes, the connection it fosters with the natural world, and how different terrains offer unique experiences, challenges, and rewards.

The Natural World: Our Best Running Partner

From east to west, coast to coast, pole to pole and from the prairies of the Midwest to the towering peaks of the Rockies, the natural world is not just a backdrop for our running adventures; it is an essential partner in our journey. There's a sense of freedom that envelops us when we tread upon the earthen trails, surrounded by the vibrant sights and sounds of nature.

Historically, humans have relied on nature not only for sustenance but also as a space for reflection, exercise, and connection. Traditional cultures across the globe have long understood the importance of nature in physical and spiritual well-being. Indigenous communities, for instance, practiced running as a way to traverse their land, find sustenance, and celebrate communal bonds. Today, we are reminded of our roots as we lace up our running shoes and embrace the wild beauty around us.

The Mental Benefits of Running in Nature

The mental rewards of running outdoors are profound and backed by science. Research has shown that spending time in nature positively affects mental health, reducing stress, alleviating symptoms of anxiety and depression, and improving overall well-being. The rhythmic pounding of your feet on the trail and the fresh air filling your lungs translates into a feeling of freedom and rejuvenation.

When you run outdoors, you're often without the distractions of daily life, no screens, no traffic jams, and no white noise. Instead, you become attuned to the rustling leaves, the chirping of birds, and the whisper of the wind. This immersion offers a unique form of mindfulness, where each stride propels you further into the present moment. The serenity of nature serves as a gentle reminder to appreciate each breath, fueling the momentum of your journey.

Discovering Different Terrains

One of the joys of running outdoors is the opportunity to explore diverse terrains, each offering a distinctive experience and set of challenges. Whether you prefer to dash along a winding path through the woods, glide over sandy beaches, or conquer rocky mountain trails, each surface brings its character and charm. Let's explore some of those different terrains in the following pages.

1. Trail Running: Trail running invites you to experience the forest's beauty firsthand. Rooted paths can be both exciting and challenging, teaching you to navigate diverse surfaces while embracing the unpredictability of nature. From the majesty of towering trees to the soft carpet of leaves underfoot, the forest becomes your companion. The trails connect you with experiences like spotting wildlife, discovering hidden streams, and marveling at breathtaking vistas. I love running through the trails, ideally with no goal or direction. Happy to explore and just be in that moment. Often the trails are my first port of call wherever I am in the world, be it Iten, Monte Gordo, Northumberland or the Middle of France. There is something about the trails that makes running something of an out of body experience.

2. Road Running: While commonly associated with urban landscapes, road running offers its unique advantages. Paved roads allow for speed and distance, enabling you to

build stamina and endurance. The familiar rhythm of pounding against asphalt creates a meditative cadence, allowing for self-reflection and goal setting. Engage with your local community as you run, finding joy in the passing conversations and interaction with neighbors.

3. Beach Running: Running alongside the shore is a symphony of sensory delights. Feel the cool sand against your feet, hear the rhythmic crashing of waves, and smell the salty sea breeze. Beach running is not just a workout; it blurs the lines between exhilaration and meditation. The uneven surface of sand challenges you to adapt, providing an invigorating workout for your legs and core while the expansive horizon offers a sense of limitless possibility. Not only is beach running speed training in disguise as well as being the perfect teacher of form and efficiency, but you also have the absolute luxury of cooling your fatigued legs off in the sea afterwards. Nature once again providing for us in our time of most need.

4. Mountain Running: For those seeking adventure, mountain running presents both beauty and intensity. The incline challenges your strength and determination, but the

reward of conquering heights reveals stunning landscapes. As you ascend, notice how the air changes—the crispness becomes invigorating, and the panoramic views provide perspective as you labor through each stride. Running trails in the mountains allows you to redefine your limits while soaking in the pristine beauty around you.

There are of course all manner of other types of running available be it over the fells, Cross-Country or even get your pretend Olympic hero vibe on and head down to your local track. I would encourage you to dip your toe in the water on as may variants as possible, after all variety is the spice of life and you never know what you might learn, who you might meet, or what you might enjoy the most. Life has a funny habit of surprising us and running is no different.

The Joys of Connecting with Nature

Running in nature is not just about physical exertion—it's also about connection. Engaging with the outdoors allows us to tap into something larger than ourselves. Each run becomes a journey of exploration, with nature as your guide.

Feel the earth beneath your feet, embracing the rawness of the connection. On trail runs, notice the unique ecosystems that flourish along your path:

the wildflowers blooming in vivid colors, the birds flitting through trees, and the babbling of brooks that accompany you as you run. Use these moments to attune your senses to the world around you, recognizing the interdependence of life.

Many runners cherish the moments when they stop to take a breath, perhaps at a scenic overlook or by a glistening riverbank. Harness that energy as a form of gratitude, reflecting on the beauty of the journey. This is something that I do a lot, even in a city center stopping momentarily to appreciate the architecture. For me this act really helps me to practice being present, which is something that I need to work to reinforce. As you breathe in the fresh air infused with the scent of pine or sea salt, allow yourself to connect deeply with the environment, embracing the sense of belonging that comes from being a part of the larger tapestry of life.

Building Community Through Nature

Running outdoors fosters connection not just with nature but also among fellow runners. Group trail runs offer opportunities to share paths, stories, and support. There's something special about conquering a mountain run or navigating a sticky trail with others—it strengthens bonds forged by the shared experience of pushing through the challenging moments together.

Many runners enjoy participating in organized group runs, workshops, or events that celebrate nature, such as charity races to protect local parks or trail clean-up initiatives. These events unite the community under a shared mission while promoting an appreciation for the environments we love to run in.

Consider collaborating with local organizations that advocate for outdoor preservation. Supporting these causes allows you to give back to the environment, creating a cycle of gratitude and connection that enriches your running experience.

Embracing Seasonal Change

June marks the peak of spring and the onset of summer, inviting a shift toward longer days and warmer temperatures. As the seasons change, so too does the nature of your running experience. Embrace the brightness of the changing weather, using it to foster exploration of new trails and terrains.

With the arrival of summer, be mindful of the sun's intensity. Adjust your running pace and hydration strategy to meet the needs of a hotter climate. Running in the early morning or late evening, when temperatures are milder, allows you to enjoy the best of what nature offers without battling heat exhaustion. Use these moments to savor the sights and sounds of nature waking or settling down, enhancing your connection to the outdoors.

The Philosophy of Slow Running

In the essence of outdoor running, consider embracing the philosophy of slow running—taking the time to absorb the beauty around you. As you move through nature, allow the experience to nourish your soul. Slow your pace to appreciate the subtleties of your environment—the sway of grasses in the wind or the intricate patterns of tree bark.

Instead of focusing solely on speed or distance, engage in a more mindful approach. Each run offers a chance to reconnect with the world around you—both within and outside. The embrace of slow running opens doors to revelations often missed in the race for pace; it encourages self-discovery and reflection on your journey.

Preparing for Outdoor Runs

To maximize the joy of running in diverse terrains, preparation is key. Equip yourself with the right mindset, gear, and strategies:

1. Choose the Right Footwear: Different terrains require specific shoes. Trail running shoes offer enhanced traction and stability, ensuring that you can navigate uneven

surfaces with confidence. Proper footwear minimizes injuries and enhances your experience.

2. Explore New Routes: Use running apps or maps to discover new trails and paths in your area. Embrace the adventure of exploration, expanding your horizons and experiencing newfound joy in familiar environments.

3. Pack Essential Gear: During longer runs, carry hydration packs or belts to ensure you remain hydrated. Consider snacks or gels for energy, especially while traversing remote paths. Safety gear, such as reflective vests, is also crucial for visibility during early morning or late-night runs.

4. Respect Nature and Follow 'Leave No Trace' Principle : Celebrate your connection to nature by respecting the wild spaces you explore. Stick to designated paths, dispose of waste responsibly, and avoid disturbing wildlife. Acknowledge that by caring for nature, you deepen your bond with the very landscapes that nurture your running practice.

Your Call to Action: Embrace the Great Outdoors

As the beauty of June unfolds, I encourage you to take actionable steps to deepen your experience with running in nature. Here are some guidelines to help you fully embrace the great outdoors:

1. Plan a Nature Run: Select a new trail or park to explore. Invite friends or fellow runners for a shared experience—create memories and strengthen connections.

2. Engage in Mindful Running: During your next outdoor run, consciously slow your pace and immerse yourself in the environment. Observe the details around you and practice gratitude for the elements that inspire you.

3. Join Group Activities: Look for local outdoor running clubs or community events that promote running in nature. Participate in group runs, workshops, or conservation efforts to connect deeply with both nature and community.

4. Document Your Journey: Consider journaling about your outdoor runs, capturing how you felt in different environments. Reflect on how these experiences impact your mood, mindset, and relationships.

5. Create Nature-Centric Goals: Set a personal goal for the month related to outdoor running—perhaps you'd like to run a certain number of trails or dedicate time to exploring varying terrains.

As you step outside into the beauty of June, allow the great outdoors to fuel your passion for running. Surrounded by the beauty of nature, embrace the lessons it teaches you about resilience, connection, and joy. Stand tall as a runner, knowing that each step you take weaves you deeper into the tapestry of life, celebrating the serene energy that carries you forward.

Embrace the journey that nature offers, recognizing that every trail runs not just through the earth, but also through your heart, igniting your spirit as you connect with the world around you. Through the power of the great outdoors, may you discover the joys of running, nurture bonds with fellow enthusiasts, and continue to flourish on this remarkable journey.

RECOVERY AND RESILIENCE

REST

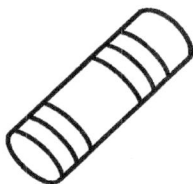

RECOVERY TECHNIQUES

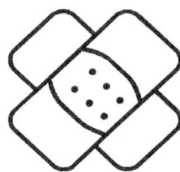

INJURY PREVENTION

JULY

Chapter 7:
JULY

Recovery and Resilience, the importance of rest and recovery techniques and preventing injuries by listening to your body.

Seasonal Reflection:

July can bring intense heat, testing your limits both physically and mentally. This is an opportunity to develop grit and determination during your runs.

Mindfulness Theme:

Use the discomfort of heat as a mindfulness tool. Focus on breath control, pacing, and how your body responds to challenges, cultivating an awareness of your strengths. Focus on staying relaxed and loose.

Mental Health Insight:

The heat of summer can sometimes lead to fatigue. Pay attention to your body's signals and remember that it's alright to adjust goals to maintain balance, ensuring mental well-being.

July Mantra:

"Rest is strength. Recovery is progress. I rise by honoring the pause."

Heat and Determination

As July unfolds, the sun shines brightly overhead, casting the world in a warm golden hue. While summer often brings an irresistible call to spend hours outdoors, pursuing adventures and logging miles, it's vital to pause and reflect on an equally important aspect of running: recovery. In this chapter, we explore the significance of rest and recovery techniques, delving into the art of listening to our bodybuilding resilience, and preventing injuries that can sideline even the most dedicated runner.

The Foundation of Recovery

In the world of running, recovery is not merely the absence of activity. Rather, it is an active and essential component of any training regimen, serving as a bedrock for performance enhancement and longevity in the sport. Just as athletes train their bodies to run faster and further, they must also train themselves to recognize when it's time to rest. I can certainly confirm from personal experience that one of the most difficult things of all, is to listen to your body and rest, to not over train. As I continue to work on connecting my mind with the miles, I believe that this is where the secret lies, reinforcing to our selves through personal mantras that it is a positive to listen to our body, and perhaps another good example is to acknowledge and celebrate the small successes when we can.

Recovery is an art that allows both body and mind to heal, adapt, and fortify for future challenges. It's during these moments of pause that the body undergoes essential repair processes, muscles recover from exertion, energy stores are replenished, and strength is rebuilt. Integrating recovery into your training regimen cultivates resilience, ensuring you don't just survive in the sport, but thrive. It is also important to remember the importance of rest to our mental health. Rest allows our minds to refresh, reflect and replenish. Taking a physical break allows our mind the opportunity to acknowledge progress, process our journey and project forward where we go from here.

The Psychological Aspect of Recovery

While physical recovery is crucial, we must not underestimate the psychological aspects of rest. Continuous training without adequate downtime can lead not only to physical fatigue but also to mental exhaustion. Compounding stress may contribute to burnout, diminished performance, and a loss of passion for running.

Embracing rest allows runners to reconnect with their love for the sport. Taking time off from structured training fosters mental clarity and the ability to approach running with renewed enthusiasm and joy. A break from routine can rekindle your motivation, shifting the focus from performance metrics to the sheer enjoyment of movement.

Additionally, the psychological boost gained from rest cannot be overstated. Mental fatigue often goes hand-in-hand with physical strain; thus, stepping back creates space for fresh perspectives and renewed vigor. You may find that after time off, you return to your running routine with a new sense of purpose and excitement, ready to tackle the challenges ahead.

Signs That You Need Rest

Understanding when to prioritize rest is critical for any runner striving for progress. Ignoring your body's signals can lead to injury, setbacks, and frustration. Here are some signs that it might be time to give your body the recovery it craves:

1. Persistent Fatigue: If the seemingly simple act of getting out of bed feels like a monumental task, it's a clear sign that your body may need a break. Training shouldn't feel like an endless cycle of exhaustion; listen to the cues your body sends.

2. Increased Irritability or Mood Swings: Emotional fluctuations can be a symptom of overtraining. If you find yourself snapping at loved ones or feeling low motivation even toward your favorite hobbies, it may be time

to step back and recharge mentally and physically.

3. Declining Performance: If you find your usual running paces slipping, and workouts feel increasingly harder, it might indicate that you're not allowing enough time for recovery. This includes monitoring heart rates during runs; if your resting heart rate rises significantly, it's an indication that your body needs a breather.

4. Regular Aches or Pains: While it's common to experience muscle soreness after intense workouts, persistent aches or pains that linger beyond the expected recovery time can signal an impending injury. Pay attention to these signals—addressing them early can prevent larger problems down the line and keep you on the path to improvement.

5. Sleep Disturbances: Troubles with sleep may indicate that your body is under stress. Recovery is integral to restoring quality sleep, so if you're struggling to fall or stay asleep, it might be time to reassess your training load. Remember that without quality sleep, your recovery processes slow, leading to a cycle of fatigue and declining performance.

Recovery Techniques to Embrace

Incorporating effective recovery techniques is essential for any runner seeking to enhance performance while minimizing the risk of injury. Here are several strategies to adopt during July's sun-soaked days:

1. Active Recovery: While complete rest has its place, engaging in low-intensity activities, such as walking, yoga, or cycling can aid recovery without the strain of regular running. Active recovery promotes blood flow, which helps transport nutrients to tired muscles, facilitating healing and alleviating soreness. I have been fortunate enough to spend some time at the High-Altitude Training Centre in Iten in Kenya, and even many of the elite Kenyan Marathon runners spend time on the exercise bike spinning away and flushing their legs.

2. Stretching and Mobility Work: Integrating stretching and mobility exercises into your recovery routine enhances flexibility, improves range of motion, and lessens the risk of injury. Consider incorporating dynamic stretches before runs and static stretching post-workout. Yoga can also be incredibly beneficial, promoting relaxation and cultivating a deeper mind-body connection.

Like many runners I have a personal hatred of stretching, I aways have. However, to combat that I have developed a 15minute Yoga routine which stretches my hip flexors, shoulders, glutes, hamstrings, back and ITB. Really its just a way that I sell stretching to my brain, but it works for me and helps to keep injury at bay.

3. Hydration and Nutrition: Adequate hydration is vital for recovery. Water helps transport nutrients and remove waste products from muscles. During Hot July runs, ensure you're replenishing electrolytes to restore balance, especially after hot, sweaty workouts. Nutritionally, focus on a balanced diet rich in carbohydrates, proteins, and healthy fats. Include foods that support muscle repair, such as lean proteins (chicken, fish, legumes), whole grains (brown rice, quinoa), and an abundance of colorful fruits and vegetables to rebuild strength and reduce inflammation.

4. Sleep: Make quality sleep a priority, aiming for seven to nine hours each night. Create a calming bedtime routine that encourages relaxation and ensure your sleeping environment is conducive to rest (cool, dark, and quiet). Quality sleep resets your body's systems, enhances muscle recovery, and

fosters mental clarity, all critical components for effective training. Like many my personal routine involves relaxing in a nice bath to wash away the stresses of the day and to clear my mind.

5. Utilize Modalities: Techniques such as ice baths, contrast baths, or compression garments can help promote recovery. Ice baths reduce inflammation, while contrast baths (alternating hot and cold water) improve circulation and alleviate soreness. Compression garments, including recovery boots, known to enhance blood flow, are a favorite among many athletes. Explore modalities that resonate with you, incorporating them as needed into your recovery routine.

6. Mindful Practices: Incorporating techniques such as meditation or deep-breathing exercises can help lower stress levels and enhance mental recovery. Taking time to relax your mind is as critical as healing your muscles, so consider dedicating a few minutes each day to mindfulness practices. The key to impactful mindful practices is consistency and routine can help with that. Routine doesn't necessarily mean doing the same thing at the same time, it can mean

having a strong process or a defined way to induce your mindfulness practice to activate whenever you need to.

The Power of Cross-Training

For some runner cross-training is a dirty phrase. I used to feel that it was cheating on my first love, running. However, increasingly for many it plays both a healthy mindset role and has a vital physical role in building resilience and reducing the risk of injury while enhancing overall fitness. By incorporating various activities into your training plan, you can engage different muscle groups, prevent overuse injuries, and allow your running muscles to rest while still staying active.

Consider activities such as swimming, which is easy on the joints but offers an excellent cardiovascular workout. Cycling is another great option, promoting leg strength and endurance without the impact of running. Additionally, Pilates or strength training focuses on core strength and stability, two crucial elements that significantly impact running performance. You don't have to replace your running days; just incorporate cross training a couple of times a week, and you'll reap the benefits while also keeping your routine enjoyable and varied.

Creating a Personalized Recovery Plan

Creating a personalized recovery plan will be unique to your needs, preferences, and training intensity. Here's how to craft your own effective recovery strategy:

1. Assess Your Training Load: Begin by evaluating your weekly running mileage and intensity. Recognize where you may need to incorporate more rest or active recovery sessions within your schedule. If you notice fatigue or discomfort, it may be time to factor more recovery into the equation.

2. Schedule Rest Days: Designate specific days in your training calendar for complete rest, ensuring they fall after particularly intense workouts. Allowing yourself scheduled rest will encourage a more mindful approach to training while keeping motivation alive.

3. Establish a Recovery Routine: Develop a routine that encompasses nutrition, hydration, mobility work, and stretching. Consider setting aside time each week specifically focused on recovery strategies to ensure you're nurturing both body and mind.

4. Track Your Progress: Maintain a training journal to log mileage, feelings of fatigue,

and recovery practices. Monitoring your responses to various recovery techniques can help refine your approach over time and lead to improved performance.

5. Listen to Your Body: Learn to tune into your physical and emotional signals. Your body holds the key to understanding its needs, so cultivate awareness to inform future training and recovery decisions. Remember that no two athletes are the same; what works for one person may not work for another.

In today's world we also have the luxury of being able to take advantage of many different types of technology. Be it a rudimentary foot massage using a golf ball, a foam roller which come in all shapes and sizes, recovery boots, a massage gun, ice baths, saunas or of course a good old sports massage. They key is to find a positive mix which is impactful to both your physical and mental recovery and enhances the overall experience of your running journey.

The Resilience Factor

Resilience is often built in the moments we least expect it—those times of recovery and adjustment. Physically, recovery strengthens your body, allowing you to return with renewed power and prowess. Mentally, the rest period refines your focus and determination, forging a mindset ready to conquer challenges.

Experiencing setbacks, whether due to injury, fatigue, or burnout, is an inevitable part of any runner's journey. Building a foundation of resilience provides you with the tools needed to navigate adversity, develop mental fortitude, and rise stronger from each setback, fostering a deeper understanding of your limits and capabilities. Develop a never give up attitude, strive to take one more step, complete one more rep, run one more km or mile. Build grit and determination into your psyche and be sure to celebrate every success that you have in relation to nurturing this new more determined focus.

Focus on cultivating resilience both in your training and in your approach to challenges. Embrace the belief that progress is not linear; the peaks and valleys along the journey contribute to the story of who you become as a runner. Every challenge faced and overcome adds depth to your journey and fuels your motivation to push through future obstacles.

The Importance of Community Support

As you navigate your individual recovery journey, consider the supportive network built within the running community. Sharing your experiences with fellow runners can foster a sense of belonging while offering encouragement and accountability. Bringing your experiences to the group encourages others to share their own challenges and triumphs, creating a safe space for open dialogue about recovery.

Encourage conversations about rest and recovery within your running circles. Organize group discussions or workshops on injury prevention and recovery strategies, inviting knowledgeable speakers such as coaches and physical therapists to share insights. Foster a culture of health that prioritizes recovery just as much as chasing personal bests.

Additionally, look for opportunities to volunteer or participate in local events promoting running safety and injury prevention. By becoming involved in the larger community, you reinforce the importance of recovery and resilience. Ultimately, a supportive community can serve as a lifeline in challenging moments, encouraging runners to prioritize health and well-being over competition.

Your Call to Action: Prioritize Recovery and Resilience

As you embrace the warmth of July, challenge yourself to prioritize recovery alongside your running pursuits. Here are actionable steps to enhance your recovery and resilience in the coming weeks:

1. Schedule Regular Rest Days: Don't shy away from taking time off to recharge. Plan your

rest days and adhere to them, letting them be a non-negotiable part of your training. If you're not ready to go cold turkey, consider implementing low-intensity days that still permit movement while allowing your body to recover. Never lose sight of the fact that it is the recovery days where the gains are made. Allowing opportunity for physical, mental and spiritual re-growth is critical.

2. Engage in Cross-Training: Explore a new fitness activity that complements your running. Experiment with swimming, cycling, or strength training to diversify your routines while allowing your running muscles to rest. Strengthen your core and reap the rewards, become more efficient, stronger and more relaxed and this will add to the enjoyment you take from running and further fuel your mental well-being.

3. Monitor Your Body: Tune in to your body's signals and practice listening actively. Embrace self-awareness to recognize when you need rest or when you're ready to push forward. If you find yourself struggling during workouts, don't hesitate to take a step back and recalculate.

4. Connect with Fellow Runners: Open discussions about recovery and build a support network within your running community. Share stories of setbacks and comebacks, highlighting the importance of rest in your journeys, and cultivate a culture of empathy and understanding.

5. Explore Recovery Techniques: Experiment with various recovery practices, be it yoga, foam rolling, or nutrition-focused efforts. Develop a routine that resonates with you, ensuring you honor your body while maximizing your performance.

As you step into the sunny days of July, remember that recovery is not just a pause; it is an integral part of your journey as a runner. Embrace the lessons of resilience that come from prioritizing rest, nurturing your body, and believing in your ability to overcome. Every step forward is a testament to the strength forged in the moments of stillness.

May your commitment to recovery and resilience guide you, ensuring that each run celebrates the joy of movement and the beauty of perseverance. As you navigate the season ahead, know that the balance of hard work and rest is what shapes you into a stronger, more resilient runner.

SETTING GOALS AND BREAKING BARRIERS

GOALS

PUSH
YOUR
LIMITS

ACHIEVABLE
GOALS

AUGUST

Chapter 8:
AUGUST

Setting goals and breaking barriers. How to set achievable goals and push your limits.

Seasonal Reflection:

As summer winds down, it's a time for reflection. Embrace the quieter moments, where rest is just as important as the miles logg

Mindfulness Theme:

Incorporate rest days mindfully into your running routine. Use these times to reflect on your journey, engage in gentle activities like yoga, or meditate while enjoying nature.

Mental Health Insight:

Acknowledge the importance of rest for mental clarity and emotional regrowth. This is a great time to recalibrate and assess your mental state and progress.

August Mantra:

"I set my sights. I trust my strength. I break through what once held me back."

Setting Goals and Breaking Barriers

As the warm summer sun begins to dip into the horizon, painting the sky in hues of orange and purple, runners gather at the local park. Some lace up their shoes for a casual jog, while others are prepared for a more serious tempo run. Regardless of their intent, they are united by a shared passion, a love for running that transcends individual goals and brings the community together. In this chapter, we will explore how to set achievable goals that push your limits while fostering connections with fellow runners. After all, the journey of running is not only about personal improvement (which is not always measured by faster times or more distance) but also about building relationships, celebrating participation, and supporting one another in performance.

The Power of Goal Setting

Setting goals can be akin to drawing a map before embarking on a journey. Without a destination, it is easy to veer off track, lose motivation, and end up wandering aimlessly. Goals give us clarity and purpose; they help define what we want to achieve and how we intend to get there.

A notable aspect of goal setting in running is the distinction between short-term and long-term goals. Short-term goals—those that can be achieved within weeks or months—help build confidence and create a sense of accomplishment. For example, committing to run three times a week or to increase your mileage by 10% this month can serve as excellent steppingstones toward greater aspirations.

Long-term goals, on the other hand, often represent a significant leap, such as preparing for a half marathon or striving to qualify for a prestigious race. These larger goals can be daunting, but they also foster a sense of aspiration and guide the direction of your training.

Furthermore, personal anecdotes can illustrate the pivotal role of goal setting within the running community. For instance, consider the story of a runner named Sarah. After struggling with her self-confidence and battling a sedentary lifestyle, Sarah decided to run her first 5K. She set a clear, achievable goal: to complete the race without walking. With each training session, Sarah not only improved her physical endurance but also found herself surrounded by a supportive group of runners from a local club. Through shared experiences and encouragement, Sarah's journey transformed from a solitary endeavor into a communal celebration of perseverance.

When setting your goals, consider using the SMART criteria, Specific, Measurable, Achievable, Relevant and Time-bound. This approach encourages clarity and structure, ensuring your goals are not only ambitious but also attainable. But it is equally important to be flexible and adaptive; life may throw unexpected challenges your way, requiring a reassessment of your original intention. Understanding that setbacks, in addition to triumphs, are part of the journey can lead to much richer experiences. There is no need to over complicate how we approach our goals, but it will be a big step in the right direction if we write them down to commit to ourselves and then reinforce that commitment by sharing them with others.

Embracing Participation

Participation is an essential value that brings people together, fueling our collective passion for running. As you set goals, remember that running is not solely a solitary endeavor. The community aspect of participation not only enhances the experience of training but also offers the motivation and support that can lead to accomplishing even the most challenging goals. Whatever personal goals that you have the experience of sharing them and discussing around them can have a hugely positive impact on your mental wellbeing and as importantly will help underpin your approach to accomplishing them by linking your mind with the miles.

Joining a local running club or inviting friends to run with you can elevate your training experience. Training groups create an environment where runners share their goals, celebrate each other's achievements, and offer encouragement during tough days. This camaraderie bolsters a sense of accountability; knowing that others are investing in their own goals can be the catalyst needed to push your own limits.

Moreover, community events, such as charity runs, local races or park runs, foster a sense of belonging. Participants often dress in matching shirts, displaying their team names or personal mottos, creating an atmosphere of shared enthusiasm. It is a beautiful sight to witness groups of people, united in a common cause, crossing finish lines together, arms raised in triumph. As you cross that finish line, take a moment to appreciate the collective effort it takes to get there. I think that we can all agree that success is even sweeter when shared with your tribe.

Additionally, participation in local races and fun runs provides opportunities to connect within the running community. While the goal may be to finish or achieve a personal record, the real victory lies in the shared experience of crossing the finish line among friends and fellow runners. It's crucial to remember that every runner has unique aspirations, and celebrating the diversity of goals is what enriches the community fabric. Some of my biggest successes have been simply making the start line. I have had many times during my life, like many of you when I have needed all of the mental fortitude possible in order to make the race and the physical element of it is never the worry, it is almost always mental.

Pushing Your Limits

While participation and community are vital, stretching beyond your comfort zone is where true growth occurs. It is easy to become complacent when repeatedly sticking to a routine, but pushing your limits opens new avenues for achievement and personal development.

To break through personal barriers, start by identifying areas that feel challenging. Perhaps you struggle to maintain a steady pace or find it difficult to tackle long runs. The key to growth is not merely to run harder but to train smarter. This requires self-awareness and a willingness to embrace discomfort as part of the journey.

Consider the journey of marathon runner Jess, who began her career as a sprinter. After setting a goal to conquer her first marathon, she realized she was accustomed to quick bursts of speed rather than sustained endurance. She faced mental barriers that were significantly amplified through her previous training. Instead of succumbing to frustration, she opted for a structured training plan that included long runs, intervals, and tempo workouts. Jess documented her journey, celebrating small wins along the way, whether it was a new distance or simply the ability to run comfortably at a faster pace.

Developing a training plan that gradually increases your intensity and distance is critical. Incorporate interval training, hill workouts, and tempo runs that challenge your cardiovascular abilities and stamina. It's through these workouts that you will confront your limits, learn to manage fatigue, and become more resilient. It is amazing how much stronger and faster people are once they can break the mental limits that the brain enforces on us.

Reflect on the history of running, legends like Steve Prefontaine and Joan Benoit Samuelson pushed not only their own limits but redefined the expectations of what runners could achieve. Their dedication to the craft serves as a reminder that barriers exist primarily in our minds; with determination and the right approach, they can be dismantled. I am a big fan of many of the Prefontaine soundbites, not least "The best pace is suicide pace and it's a good day to die" The thing I love about this is that it removes any consideration of mental limits or barriers.

Nature as a Companion

As you embark on the journey of goal setting and breaking barriers, consider seeking inspiration from the world around you. Nature can be a powerful companion during your runs, providing both a serene backdrop and a motivating force. From the simple rustling of leaves to the exhilarating sound of waves crashing, immersing yourself in nature offers perspective and rejuvenation. Sometimes the simple act of using nature as a distraction is enough to recenter us, bring rewards and sometimes can even bring a big breakthrough.

As discussed in earlier chapters, running in different environments, whether it's a forest trail, beachside path, or city streets, As can influence your training in remarkable ways. For instance, trail runs may challenge your agility and focus on a way that road running does not, helping to develop adaptability and strength. By varying your routes and engaging with diverse landscapes, you allow your mind and body to break free from the constraints of a routine, fostering creativity in your training strategy.

Moreover, nature reminds us of the world's interconnectedness. Each run can be a reflection on your place within it, urging you to be more mindful of your surroundings. The birds, the trees, the changing seasons, each element offers a lesson about resilience and perseverance. When setting your goals, consider integrating environmental mindfulness into your journey. Perhaps you aim to run in a new national park, participate in a race for a cause, or engage in a clean-up as a community on your runs.

An inspiring story of a runner named Tom illustrates this beautifully. Tom, an avid nature enthusiast, decided to run a series of races across different national parks. Each race would be coupled with a mission—cleaning up a designated area in the park before or after the event. Over time, not only did Tom achieve personal fitness goals, but he also connected with various communities through his conservation efforts. Nature was not just a backdrop; it became an integral part of his mission, tying his love for running with his passion for the environment. In Toms case, this reinforced his sense of enjoyment from running by giving it even more purpose.

Celebrating Progress

A crucial aspect of setting goals is acknowledging progress along the way. It's important not to focus solely on the finish line; every small victory is worth celebrating. This recognition fuels motivation and cultivates an attitude of gratitude for the journey itself. It is important to work on process-based goals rather than outcome-based goals alone.

Document your progress, whether in a running journal, an app, or through social media channels, and don't hesitate to share milestones with your running community. Celebrate every new distance conquered, every personal record achieved, and even the days when you showed up at the start despite feeling less than motivated. Engaging in these reflections will reinforce the value of your efforts and the importance of the collective journey.

Consider hosting a small gathering after achieving a significant goal. Invite friends, family, and fellow runners to share in your celebration. Create a space for everyone to talk about their own journeys, fostering an environment where stories of struggle and success are openly exchanged. This collective celebration strengthens bonds and promotes a culture of support among runners.

By sharing your progress with others, you also inspire them to pursue their goals. There's a unique energy that arises when we witness others striving to achieve their aspirations. Take the time to celebrate not only your own accomplishments but also those of your fellow runners. As you foster a supportive environment, you contribute to a thriving running community where everyone feels empowered to pursue their ambitions.

Breaking Through Mental Barriers

Setting and achieving goals is not only a physical endeavor; it's as much, if not more, a mental one. Mental barriers can prove more daunting than physical ones, often leading to self-doubt and hesitation. Pushing past these challenges requires self-compassion and a willingness to examine your mindset.

Explore techniques such as visualization and positive affirmations. Visualizing yourself successfully meeting your goal can create a powerful mental image that pushes you to realize it. During training, envision the moment of crossing the finish line, feeling the rush of pride and accomplishment. Use affirmations to reinforce your commitment and confidence: phrases like "I am capable," or "I can do hard things" These can help to frame your mindset and dispel negativity.

Another powerful technique involves mindfulness and meditation. Many elite athletes incorporate mindfulness practices into their routines to enhance focus and clarity. As you run, take the time to tune into your breath, your body's movements, and the environment surrounding you. This present-moment awareness can reduce anxiety and help in processing the challenges you face.

Additionally, it's vital to understand that setbacks are a natural part of the running journey. Not every training session will go as planned, nor will every race culminate in the desired results. Learning to appreciate the process rather than solely focusing on the outcome fosters resilience and fortitude.

Engage in self-reflection after challenging moments. Analyze what went wrong, take lessons from the experience, and determine how they can inform your strategy moving forward. The ability to recover from setbacks, both physically and mentally, will ultimately define your progress as a runner and the extent to which you can push your limits.

Conclusion: A Journey Beyond the Finish Line

As you navigate the complexities of setting goals and breaking barriers, remember that running is more than just personal achievement; it is a shared experience that binds the community together. Each step you take presents an opportunity to connect with the world around you, to celebrate your love for the sport, and to inspire others to embrace their own journeys.

Set goals that resonate with your values and aspirations, leverage the collective power of participation, and never shy away from pushing your boundaries. In the fabric of running, every thread contributes to a tapestry of shared experiences, connections, and enduring resilience.

As you lace up your shoes, take a moment to breathe in the world around you. Embrace the journey, foster connections, push your limits, and most importantly, enjoy the run. Onward, fellow runner—your path is waiting.

With every stride, remember: the finish line is just a waypoint on a much larger course. Your adventures in running are only beginning, and the road ahead is filled with both challenges and triumphs. Embrace them, learn from them, and let them inspire you to continue moving forward—one step at a time.

August Call to Action: Set the Goal, Trust the Stride

August is your invitation to turn reflection into action. Set a goal that challenges you—and commit to showing up for it, one run at a time. Not to chase perfection, but to discover your resilience, your rhythm, and your strength.

Your August Goal Snapshot

What do I want to achieve this month?

Why does it matter to me?

When will check in with myself?

Tip: Keep it realistic. Keep it meaningful. Keep it yours.

Breakthrough, Not Burnout

If the goal feels too big some days—adjust, don't abandon. Progress is not about doing it all. It's about doing something.

Mantra to repeat mid-run:

"This is part of it. I keep moving forward."

Track One Win a Week

Week 1:

Week 2:

Week 3:

Week 4:

Even small steps count. Especially small steps. This is not about the finish line; it's about becoming someone who shows up. So set your goal. Take the first step. Let August be the month you prove to yourself: You are much stronger than the voice that doubts you.

RUNNING THROUGH LIFE'S CHALLENGES

CLEAR YOUR MIND

BUILD YOUR RESILIENCE

FIND CALM

SEPTEMBER

Chapter 9:
SEPTEMBER

Running through life's challenges, using running as a tool for coping with stress and adversity

Seasonal Reflection:

September marks the transition into fall. The changing leaves are symbolic of change, reminding you of your evolving relationship with running.

Mindfulness Theme:

Pay attention to the sensory experiences of running through autumn landscapes—the crunch of leaves, the scent of fresh air. Each element reinforces your connection to the present. Feel the colling temperatures and the breeze on your face as a mental reminder to check in with yourself.

Mental Health Insight:

Shift your focus from external goals to internal growth. Reflect on what you have learned through each season and how you have changed, acknowledging both struggles and successes. How does this make you feel?

September Mantra:

"Through every storm, I run. I breathe through the weight. I find strength in the struggle."

Running Through Life's Challenges

As the crisp autumn air begins to settle in, the world transforms into a tapestry of golden leaves and vibrant sunsets. September is not just another month; it symbolizes a transition, where summer's warmth gives way to the reflective beauty of fall. For many runners, this month also represents a chance to reconnect with themselves, harnessing the power of each step to navigate through life's myriad challenges. In this chapter, we will explore how running serves as an invaluable tool for coping with stress and adversity, ultimately leading to personal growth and resilience.

The Intersection of Running and Mental Health

Running is more than just a physical activity. It acts as a profound tool for enhancing mental well-being. Research consistently highlights the mental health benefits derived from regular physical activity, particularly running. The endorphins released during exercise, often referred to as "feel-good hormones," can lead to a natural high, reducing feelings of anxiety and depression.

Each step taken down a winding path or city street can echo the struggles we face in life. When dealing with challenging moments, it can often feel overwhelming, like trying to navigate an insurmountable mountain.

However, through running, we develop coping mechanisms that allow us to tackle adversity with a clearer mindset.

For instance, consider the story of Maya, a dedicated runner who found solace in her daily workouts after the passing of her mother. Initially, the weight of grief was all-consuming, isolating her from friends and family and amplifying her feelings of sorrow. Yet, as she laced up her running shoes and hit the pavement, the rhythm of her feet striking the ground began to provide a sense of relief. Each run transformed her sadness into a meditative journey, allowing her to process her emotions while immersing herself in nature's beauty.

It's essential to understand that the relationship between running and mental health is bi-directional; while running improves mental well-being, mental health also influences our capacity to run. When we experience stress or emotional turbulence, our motivation can dip, making it more challenging to stick to our running routine. Being aware of this interplay encourages us not only to maintain our physical activity but also to address our mental health directly. Consistency is the key to growth, motivation will come and go, but showing up daily with intention and purpose will significantly strengthen your mental and physical health and will help to link them in a positive way.

Establishing a Routine

Creating a consistent running routine can be one of the most effective ways to manage stress. When life feels chaotic, having a designated time to run can bring structure and predictability. This routine can be a grounding force, offering you a reliable outlet to channel your emotions—be it anger, sadness, or frustration.

Setting a schedule, even when facing challenging life events, can create a sense of normality. For instance, if you're coping with a stressful job or personal situation, allotting 30 minutes each morning or evening for a run can serve as your designated "me-time." Over time, this commitment to yourself becomes a sanctuary, a sacred space where life's challenges briefly fade into the background. On a personal level this has saved my sanity on many occasions over the years, even if I have not managed the full 30minutes even a few moments can make a positive impact and help you to focus on your positive intention.

Marissa, an educator in a demanding school, found that squeezing in a run during her lunch break revitalized her both physically and mentally. As she stepped outside for those precious moments alone, the sounds of laughter and chatter faded, replaced by the rhythmic sound of her breath. It was during these intervals that she found the clarity to approach the challenges presented by her students with renewed energy and patience.

To establish a routine that sticks, it's helpful to plan. Choose your running days and times and mark them on your calendar as you would any important appointment. Additionally, prepare your running gear the night before. Having your shoes and clothes ready to go removes barriers to your commitment and sets a positive tone for the day ahead. Whilst I don't manage to do this before every run, I frequently spend a few moments before a workout thinking deeply what I am hoping to achieve from the run and reinforcing the commitment to myself that I have the grit to get it done. On some days, this can turn into a positive manifestation meditation that I use if the run is a challenging one.

The Power of Nature

In today's fast-paced world, it's easy to overlook the therapeutic effects of nature. The mere act of running outdoors can ground us and remind us how interconnected we are with the world around us. Whether it's through the rustling of leaves, the gentle sway of branches, or the sight of wildlife, nature offers a refreshing perspective on life's challenges.

I live in the countryside and there are many occasions when I can run alongside deer, past lambs or watch red kite or other birds of prey soar over me high in the sky. These often-fleeting connections with nature are truly powerful and more than anything, they remind me of my privilege in being able to run, they remind me that I run because I choose to and not because I must.

When Josh was faced with the stressful decision to change career paths after years of feeling unfulfilled, he turned to the trails near his home for clarity. Each run steeped in the beauty of colorful foliage and fresh air helped him work through his thoughts more intuitively. Running amidst nature became a process of reflection as he contemplated his next steps. The constant flow of his breath was harmonized with his thoughts, creating a flow state where answers often revealed themselves. Josh was able to clear his mind and make a decision that he was comfortable with.

Furthermore, scientific studies have shown that spending time in green spaces can significantly reduce cortisol levels—the body's primary stress hormone. Therefore, if you can, choose routes that take you through parks, forests, or other natural settings. This simple shift in your running environment can amplify the mental health benefits of your runs.

In addition, consider instilling a practice of mindfulness during your outdoor runs. Pay attention to your surroundings, the sounds of the birds singing, the aroma of pine, or wild garlic, or even the feeling of the breeze against your skin. Embracing these sensory experiences can cultivate a sense of gratitude and connection to the present moment, further enhancing the calming effects of your run. All of these experiences help to give purpose to your runs and will make it even easier to pull on those trainers and get into your run.

Fostering a Growth Mindset

Life's challenges are an inevitable part of the human experience. The way we respond to these challenges can define our growth. Adopting a growth mindset, an understanding that abilities and intelligence can be developed through dedication and hard work, can fundamentally change how we view adversity. Running will not only energize and re-invigorate us but will help us with gratitude, reminding us once again that we are lucky to be able to run and that we do so because we choose to.

Running is a powerful metaphor for this principle. Each new distance, pace, or terrain challenges you to grow, pushing you beyond your perceived limits. The discomfort felt during a tough workout can mirror the discomfort of facing life challenges. However, just as you learn to navigate the physical elation of pushing through a long run, so too can you learn to persevere through adversity.

Consider the example of Alex, a runner who faced severe anxiety during high school. He took up running to channel his worries into physical activity, setting small, achievable goals for himself. As he began to conquer those goals, running his first mile without stopping, completing a 5K, and eventually a half marathon, he learned that he was capable of more than he ever believed. Each accomplishment built his confidence and reshaped his mindset. Instead of viewing obstacles as insurmountable walls, he began to see them as hurdles to be cleared with persistence and patience.

This shift in perception can also be applied outside of running. Whether you're facing personal, professional, or emotional challenges, embracing them as opportunities for growth will allow you to cultivate resilience. Acknowledge that setbacks are often the precursors to breakthroughs; just as in running, the most profound growth often happens when we resist the urge to give up.

To cultivate a growth mindset, practice self-compassion during difficult runs or challenging life moments. Understand that setbacks are not reflections of your worth, they are opportunities for learning and growth. When you encounter a tough run, instead of beating yourself up for not meeting your expectations, remind yourself that every runner has struggled at some point. Treat yourself with the same kindness you would offer a friend facing a tough time.

Building Resilience Through Challenges

Running inherently teaches resilience. The physical training required to improve endurance parallels the mental strength needed to face life's difficulties. Each time you lace up your shoes and hit the pavement, you're inherently battling against your own limits, both physical and mental. You are learning to embrace discomfort, building resilience that extends far beyond the confines of your running shoes.

Samantha, a marathon runner, faced a sudden health crisis that forced her to take a step back from her training. Instead of resigning herself to defeat, she focused on what she could control: her mindset and her recovery. Drawing on the lessons of resilience that running had instilled in her, she committed to her rehabilitation process, setting recovery goals that mirrored her training regimen. Each goal reached during her recovery felt monumental, serving as reminders that while challenges can temporarily sidetrack us, they don't define us. I have been fortunate to attend several key notes speaches given by the high perfomance podcast host Jake Humphrey, and he talks frequently about being the light in the room. I really believe that this positive focus, taking a glass half full rather than a glass half empty approach can have significant impact on both your mental health and your running experiences. Each challenge is an opportunity for us to find out more about ourselves and in my view that is something to be thankful for.

Moreover, it's essential to understand that resilience is not about avoiding adversity but rather learning how to respond to it. This involves developing coping strategies, building a support system, and maintaining a positive outlook. Use your running community as a resource; share your struggles, rely on others, and strengthen your support network. Many runners have unique stories of overcoming challenges, and their experiences can inspire and motivate you during your own hardships.

As you encounter life's hurdles, remember that every challenge presents an opportunity to grow stronger. Just as you may push through the last few miles of a long run, you can muster the courage to navigate through adversity. Build your resilience through this understanding, it is a skill that can be cultivated and strengthened over time. Remember the best time to begin this practice is right now, not today, but right now in this very moment.

Mindfulness and Reflection During Running

The practice of mindfulness—being fully present in the moment—can be integrated into your running routine to combat stress and anxiety. As you run, focus on your breath, the cadence of your steps, and the sensation of the ground beneath your feet. Reflect on your thoughts without judgment, allowing them to flow in and out like a stream. Find an approach that works for you, a thought, a feeling or a mantra. I often repeat over and over: "Tranquillo, Tranquillo".

Sarah, a former athlete turned mindfulness enthusiast, utilizes her runs as a time for meditation. Each time she hits the pavement, she consciously sets aside her worries and cultivates gratitude for the moment. By concentrating on the rhythm of her body and the world around her, she finds a sanctuary where stress dissipates, leaving only clarity and gratitude in its place.

This practice is not limited to the tranquil trails or peaceful parks. Even urban runs can serve as environments for mindfulness. As you navigate busy streets, practice focusing on the sights, sounds, and sensations of your surroundings, notice the laughter of children, the buzz of commuters, or the warmth of the sun on your face. Embracing mindfulness during your runs can create a mental refuge from the chaos of life.

Consider using specific mantras or affirmations during your runs to enhance your mindfulness practice. Phrases like "I am strong," "I can handle this," or "This too shall pass" can create mental anchors that help refocus your thoughts when they begin to drift toward negativity or stress.

Setting Realistic Goals During Tough Times

In the face of adversity, it can be difficult to maintain motivation and consistency. let alone reach for ambitious running goals. However, it's essential to set realistic expectations and adjust them to suit your current circumstances. There's beauty in small victories; sometimes it's not about how far you run but rather having the courage to lace up your shoes and step outside. Do not make that front door into something it is not, open it, breath in the air and take in the sights and then just like every other time, your run will start by putting one foot in front of the other. Intention is everything.

When faced with intense stress, it may feel daunting to train for a marathon. Instead, focus on shorter distances or even simple routines, such as committing to a 10-minute daily walk or run. Acknowledge these efforts without harsh judgment. Each goal, no matter how small, contributes to your resilience. During times of high stress, or low moods, it is more important than ever to log your activity, your feelings and also to embrace your community, though you will likely find in times like these, that they are already there leaning in for you and ready to support wherever and however they can.

James, who struggled with job loss, turned to running to cope. He initially set an intention of running every day for just 15 minutes, regardless of pace or distance. This manageable goal allowed him to build a routine without overwhelming pressure. Over time, he found that the structure provided by these runs not only lifted his mood but encouraged him to pursue new job opportunities more positively. This simple act of running helps to give us purposes, reminds us of our intention and can greatly improve our self-esteem, remember to continue to celebrate small victories.

Consider journaling your goals and reflecting on your progress. Writing down your achievements, no matter how minor, can serve as a reminder of your capacity to overcome challenges. This technique of tracking even the smallest victories create a tangible sense of accomplishment that can motivate you to continue pursuing self-improvement.

Creating a Supportive Environment

Community plays a crucial role in overcoming challenges. Surround yourself with supportive individuals who can uplift you during difficult times. Seek out running clubs or groups that foster camaraderie and motivation. Having others to share your journey with can make a profound difference, especially during life's struggles. I often talk about being a net additive to a room, take an interest in people and their lives, project energy and authenticity. You will find that if you are able to show your intention in this way that you attract positive people who will reflect your energy, share your authenticity and be net additives to your life.

Emily, who faced a health crisis that limited her ability to run long distances, found strength in reaching out to her local running community. They welcomed her with open arms, appreciating every effort she made, no matter how small. The support she received inspired her to participate in local group runs, gradually increasing her confidence while reminding her that she was not alone in her journey. The running community are kind and will embrace you. Like many, I will personally run with anyone of any ability and often have, from first time run/walkers, those returning from serious injury through to national champions, Olympians and even world record holders.

You may also consider adding a virtual aspect to your support system. Social media can be a useful tool for connecting with like-minded runners facing similar challenges. Sharing your journey online can provide encouragement and motivation, and you might be surprised at the number of people who resonate with your experiences. Building this network can foster connection and create lasting relationships that inspire personal growth.

In addition to joining groups, consider utilizing online platforms that offer running challenges or community events. Participating in virtual races, for instance, can provide you with motivation and a sense of achievement even while going through tough times. These connections can serve as powerful reminders of the shared experiences within the running community.

Concluding Thoughts: Running as a Lifeline

As September unfolds and the beauty of autumn envelops us, let running serve as more than just a means of exercise; let it be a lifeline during life's challenges. Through every step, you can confront your adversities, drawing from the well of resilience that you've cultivated during countless miles. Feel every step revitalize the blood racing through your veins, let every heartbeat reinforce of your strength and courage and allow every breath to remind you of the deep connections you are building through your growing running community.

Remember that running can provide a sanctuary for processing emotions, a space for fostering mindfulness, and a catalyst for embracing growth. Engage with the community, set realistic goals, and empower yourself to navigate challenges with determination and courage.

As the leaves fall and the air cools, take a moment to reflect on your journey. Celebrate how far you have come and embrace the lessons learned along the way. Life may present obstacles, but running equips you with the tools to meet these challenges head-on. With each stride, you discover not just the strength in your legs, the resilience in your heart and the intention and commitment in your mind.

So, as you step outside this September, breathe in the autumn air, soak in the beauty of the season, and run boldly into the challenges life brings your way. After all, it is your journey that shapes you, and every mile is a testament to your strength and endurance.

Embracing Every Journey

In our day-to-day lives, we often focus on the destination—the goals we aim to achieve, the milestones we seek to reach. Similarly, in running, it's easy to get fixated on race times or distances. But the true essence lies not only in the finish line but also in the process and the journey each runner undertakes. Each run, each hurdle, is an opportunity for personal discovery.

The diversity of experiences within the running community exemplifies this notion. Some runners enter competitions, while others use running as a means of escape or self-reflection. On many occasions I have gone years without entering a race and as I sit here and right this, whilst I hope to enter a race soon, it has been over 2 years since I pulled on a race number. However, that never detracts from my love of running or appreciation for all the things that it brings to me. Sometimes racing is part of my journey and sometimes it is not and because I focus on process goals over outcome goals all is well. No matter the motivation, the act of being physically active translates into emotional resilience. Whether you are running through serene landscapes or navigating through the bustling city, every run contributes to shaping your identity and fortifying your spirit.

Your journey in running, much like life, may have its highs and lows. Celebrate every accomplishment and learn from each setback. Take pride in your ability to keep moving forward, both literally and metaphorically.

As we end September and transition into the cooler months ahead, remember running is more than a workout; it can be an essential ally in your quest to navigate life's challenges. May each step you take be empowered by purpose, wisdom, and resilience, reminding you that you have the strength to run through every challenge that comes your way.

September Call to Action: Run Toward the Challenge

This month, do not run from the hard things, run through them.

Let every mile remind you that you're capable of showing up for yourself, even when life feels heavy. Lace up with intention. Step outside with purpose. Whether you're logging one mile or ten, know that your effort is a radical act of strength, resilience, and hope.

YOUR SEPTEMBER CHALLENGE

- *Pick a Personal Challenge*
  Something you're currently navigating (grief, stress, burnout, fatigue, indecision, change)

- *Dedicate a Run to It*
  Use the run to process, not to avoid Carry it with you, then let it go, step by step.

- *Reflect After Your Run*
  Write one sentence: How did I feel? What shifted?

October

THE RUNNER'S JOURNEY

Exploring personal growth and the transformative power of running

Chapter 10:
OCTOBER

The runner's journey, exploring personal growth and the transformative power of running.

Seasonal Reflection:

October brings a rich tapestry of colors. It's a month for harvesting both literal produce and the rewards of your training. Physical, mental, emotional and spiritual.

Mindfulness Theme:

Use your runs as an opportunity to practice gratitude, appreciate the beauty around you, from the foliage to the crisp air, and recognize the bounty of your hard work.

Mental Health Insight:

Acknowledge the importance of celebrating your victories, big and small. Reflect on how running has contributed to your overall sense of happiness and fulfillment. Think of specific examples and reflect what they mean to you.

October Mantra:

"With every run, I uncover more of who I am becoming."
"My journey is not just in miles, but in meaning."

The Runner's Journey

As the days grow shorter and the air turns brisk, October ushers in a season of reflection and transformation. The vibrant hues of fall leaves remind us that change is not only inevitable but a beautiful part of the human experience. Just like the trees shedding their leaves, we too can embrace transformation, especially in the context of running. Every mile we log, every challenge we face, and every goal we set can lead us on a profound journey of personal growth.

In this chapter, we will explore the transformative power of running and how it contributes to our self-discovery, resilience, and overall well-being. Through stories of individuals who have experienced significant change through their running journeys, we will uncover the myriad ways in which running shapes us into the people we are meant to become.

Running as a Catalyst for Change

I am hopeful that if you have made it this far, that like me you will agree that running is so much more than just exercise; it is a profound teacher. The physical act of running often brings about change in our mental, emotional, and spiritual selves. Each run presents an opportunity to push our limits, confront our fears, and ultimately grow. It can serve as a launching pad for significant personal transformation, inviting us to step beyond the confines of our comfort zones.

Consider the journey of David, a once sedentary individual who found himself at a crossroads in his life. After years of neglecting his health and feeling increasingly detached from his well-being, he decided to lace up his running shoes on a whim. What began as an attempt to drop a few pounds transformed into a lifelong commitment to personal growth.

David's story is not uncommon. Many individuals come to running seeking physical change, only to find that the greatest transformations occur within. As he started training for his first 5K, David encountered more than just physical challenges—the mental hurdles proved equally daunting. He learned to confront the voices of doubt that emerged during arduous training sessions. The simple act of running slowly turned into a deeper examination of his beliefs about his capabilities. Each finish line was not just a testament to physical endurance but also a celebration of his evolving self-worth.

Embracing Vulnerability in Running

Running encourages vulnerability, particularly when we expose ourselves to the elements, pushing ourselves emotionally and physically. To transform, we must first be willing to acknowledge our fears and insecurities. The act of putting one foot in front of the other amid discomfort fosters a unique environment for vulnerability.

When Maria decided to train for a marathon after overcoming a tumultuous period in her life, she embarked on a journey of emotional healing. Every run was a confrontation with past traumas and the insecurities that accompanied them. As she battled through moments of doubt, she learned that vulnerability does not equate to weakness; rather, it became a source of strength.

During training, Maria encountered countless challenges, from injuries to emotional setbacks. Instead of shying away from these experiences, she embraced them, recognizing that they were part of her journey. Each time she ran through the discomfort, she found herself building resilience—the ability to rise above her circumstances. This newfound strength not only helped her navigate her training but also enabled her to face other facets of her life with renewed courage.

Being vulnerable on our running journey, sharing our struggles, setbacks, and victories, can also foster connections with others. It is also a big part of what makes us authentic. The running community is filled with individuals who have faced their own challenges. Sharing stories creates a bond that emphasizes our shared experiences, allowing us to realize we are not alone in our struggles. Encouraging others to embrace their vulnerability can ultimately lead to collective growth. I encourage you to once again remind yourself that you run because you can, because you choose to, not because you have to.

Goal Setting: From Ordinary to Extraordinary

Setting goals is an integral part of any running journey. However, the process of setting and pursuing goals extends beyond mere physical achievements. It serves as a framework for self-improvement and a pathway to transformation. When we set goals that stretch our limits, we summon courage and determination to pursue greatness.

In October, as the weather beckons us to run, reflect on your own goals. Are they merely numbers, the pace of your run or the distance you cover? Or do they delve deeper, providing insight into your character and personal growth? The most rewarding goals often encompass holistic development rather than solely physical benchmarks.

Take the experience of Jamal, who, after struggling with self-doubt and anxiety, set a goal that seemed inconceivable: to run a half marathon. At first, his friends and family were skeptical, citing his previous struggle to run even a mile. However, Jamal saw this as an opportunity to grow beyond the limitations he had placed on himself.

As he trained, he set smaller interim goals, steppingstones if you will, completing a mile without stopping, gradually increasing his distance, and picking up speed. Each accomplishment fueled his motivation, but what he gained through the process surpassed any physical distance covered. He learned perseverance through the early morning runs when the world remained quiet, the power of accountability through training groups, and the joy of celebrating small victories with others.

By focusing on meaningful goals rather than solely finishing the race, Jamal cultivated resilience, courage, and self-belief. His journey inspired peers, showing them that the process of working toward a goal is as vital, if not more so, than achieving the goal itself. Once more re-iterating the importance of process goals over outcome only based goals.

The Community Impact: Running Together, Growing Together

As we navigate our personal journeys through running, it is vital to acknowledge the significance of community. The support we receive from fellow runners can amplify our transformation. Whether through a local running club or online running forum, sharing our challenges, triumphs, and experiences with others fosters a sense of belonging and encouragement.

The power of community is evident in the impact of organized runs and charity races. Marathons and fun runs often serve as platforms for individuals to come together, share their stories, and promote causes they are passionate about. These events create a collective sense of purpose and unity, emphasizing that personal growth often intersects with communal growth.

Take the story of the Sunshine Running Group, a local club dedicated not only to running but also to uplifting and supporting its members through their personal journeys. When Rachel joined the group, she was hesitant and unsure of her abilities, but the encouraging atmosphere welcomed her. As each member shared their struggles, be it overcoming injury, dealing with personal loss, or simply finding motivation, the community developed a profound bond.

Over time, Rachel not only improved her running skills but also found joy in supporting others. By taking on a mentorship role for new members, she experienced personal growth that transcended her own running journey. Helping others discover their strength created a ripple effect. Rachel's confidence flourished, and witnessing the transformation of those around her brought her deep fulfillment.

When we embrace the collective aspect of running, we learn that personal growth is not a solitary endeavor. Together, we can uplift one another, offering encouragement, perspective, and strength through our shared experiences. This sense of community fosters resilience and amplifies the transformative power of running.

Mindfulness on the Run

Amid our training and races, it is easy to get lost in the rush to achieve our goals. Taking time to practice mindfulness during our runs can deepen our connection to ourselves and the world around us. While we focus on our pace or distance, we can also connect with our thoughts and emotions, uncovering layers of personal growth along the way.

Practicing mindfulness during running involves actively engaging with our surroundings, paying attention to breath, and noticing our thoughts without judgment. This mindfulness practice can be a powerful tool for self-reflection and personal growth.

For instance, while on a long run through a wooded path, consider how the natural elements symbolize change and resilience. The leaves may fall, but new growth will emerge in due season. This awareness of nature's cycles can mirror our experience in life, acknowledging that all things change and that we too can rise again after challenges.

Jessica, an experienced runner, discovered the power of mindfulness when training for her biggest race yet. Along her routes, she changed her focus from merely logging miles to appreciating the tranquility of her surroundings. With each run, she punched the reset button on her mind, allowing clarity and calmness to seep into her thoughts. By the time race day approached, Jessica had not only improved her physical readiness but also cultivated a sense of emotional peace that enabled her to enjoy the experience fully.

Practicing mindfulness during running can serve as a form of meditation, providing clarity and renewed purpose. It allows us to lean into our thoughts, acknowledge our feelings, and process our experiences, ultimately leading to personal growth. Not to mention a deeper sense of fulfillment, purpose and gratitude.

The Journey of Self-Discovery

The transformative power of running catalyzes a journey of self-discovery, unlocking our inner potential and illuminating aspects of ourselves we may never have explored. Every run can serve as a metaphorical mirror, reflecting our strengths, weaknesses, fears, and triumphs. Embracing this journey can lead to life-altering realizations.

Consider the transformative story of Lauren, who approached running as a means of escape from the demands of her busy life. Initially, she used to run to avoid stress, but as she began to dig deeper into her motivations, she uncovered layers of personal insight that prompted profound changes.

Through deliberate self-reflection during her runs, Lauren began to understand her relationship with stress and anxiety. Rather than avoiding them, she learned to confront and process these emotions as she distanced herself from her struggles, one step at a time. With every mile conquered, she witnessed her fears transform into enthusiasm. Ultimately, this self-discovery helped Lauren define her values and take bold steps in her career and personal life. Running gave Lauren the confidence to believe in herself.

Running illuminated her path, showcasing that every journey begins with a willingness to explore both the terrain outside and within oneself. As we lace up our shoes and embark on our runs, we embark not just on a physical journey but on an exploration of our authentic selves.

Reflection and Gratitude: Celebrating the Journey

As October unfolds, it encourages us to reflect on our journeys and express gratitude for the changes that running has inspired within us. Reflecting allows us to appreciate how far we have come, identify areas for growth, and commit to continuing our journey with intention.

At the end of the month, consider taking time to journal about your running experiences. Ask yourself:

- What challenges did I overcome, and how did they shape me?

- What goals have I accomplished that extend beyond physical achievements?

- How have I grown as a person, and how can I continue this journey?

This practice of reflection fosters self-awareness and integrates the lessons learned along the way. It ultimately cultivates a mindset of gratitude, a vital component of personal growth.

Imagine Mary, a runner reflecting on her journey throughout October. After completing her first half marathon, she took the time to express gratitude not only for her achievement but also for the personal growth fostered throughout her training. She acknowledged the struggles, the moments of self-doubt, physical exhaustion, and emotional breakthroughs, and recognized their role in shaping her character. The challenges really do become opportunities in disguise once we learn to slightly adjust the lens from which we view them, and running can really help us to do that.

Mary's reflections inspired her to share her journey with others, emphasizing the importance of celebrating not just the outcome but every step taken to reach it. By fostering a culture of gratitude and reflection, members of her running group learned to embrace their journeys more deeply, creating a supportive environment ripe for personal transformation.

Conclusion: Embracing Ongoing Transformation

As the October breeze ushers in a season of introspection, remember that running serves as a powerful vehicle for transformation. It invites us to confront our limits, embrace our vulnerabilities, set meaningful goals, and build a supportive community. The journey of personal growth through running is never-ending; it is an ongoing opportunity for self-discovery, resilience, and renewal.

Through running, we can redefine who we are and who we can become. As we lace up our shoes and forge ahead on this remarkable journey, let us carry with us the transformative lessons learned along the way. Embrace the changes, remain open to growth, and traverse the path forward with courage and grace.

October may signal the end of one season, but it also dawns the promise of new beginnings. Whether scaling the heights of personal achievements or navigating the valleys of challenge, every mile traveled is a testament to the strength, resilience, and boundless potential within us.

As we embark on this journey together, may our hearts be filled with gratitude and our minds be open to the beauty of transformation that the running experience affords us. Every run leads us toward a deeper understanding of ourselves, encouraging both personal growth and endless possibilities.

So, this October, let running be not just a physical pursuit but a profound odyssey of the heart, soul, and mind, a journey that forever alters the way we view ourselves and the world around us.

Call to Action: Run the Change. Become the Journey

The leaves are turning. So are you. Let October be the month you stop chasing outcomes and start becoming through every step.

This is not just about running. It's about becoming more of who you already are and taking positive strides towards continuing to explore and ultimately discover our authentic selves.

1. Shed the doubts.
2. Embrace the questions.
3. Set the kind of goals that make your soul sit up straighter.

Remember that You don't need to have it all figured out. You just need to keep moving with intention. Reflect on the transformation you've already sparked, honor the path that has shaped you and step into the unknown with open hands and a willing heart.

Running does not just change your body; it can rewire your brain, and it often rewrites your story. So go ahead: Lace up. Let go. Lean in. You are already creating the next version of you and with every positive intention, every fulfilled commitment, every manifestation or meditation and every step brings you closer to that authentic version of yourself. Remember to have fun with it and further strengthen your community by sharing your progress with your community.

Reflecting on achievements and milestones, big or small.

- Progress made
- Goals achieved
- How far I've come
- Lessons learned

November

Chapter 11:

NOVEMBER

Celebrating successes. Reflecting on achievements and milestones big and small.

Seasonal Reflection:

November signifies the onset of winter and prompts thoughts of change. The waning daylight can be a time of introspection.

Mindfulness Theme:

Run in the fading light, focusing on the transition. Allow your thoughts to settle as you observe the shifts around you, both in nature and where you are in your journey.

Mental Health Insight:

As the weather cools, potential feelings of isolation may arise. Lean into the community and support around you; connect with fellow runners and share your experiences.

November Mantra:

"Success is not just the finish line, it is every step, every stride, every moment, keep going."

Celebrating Successes

As November arrives, with its crisp air and vibrant foliage, it invites us to take a moment to pause and reflect on our journey, use this opportunity to take stock of the victories and the milestones that define us. This chapter serves as a reminder to acknowledge our accomplishments, whether they are monumental achievements or quiet victories. In the context of running, celebration is not just about finishing races; it extends to every training session completed, every hurdle overcome, and every personal discovery made along the way. Including those days when you made the choice to lace up your running shoes when it would have been easier to stay indoors.

In this chapter, we will explore the importance of recognizing and celebrating successes in our running journey. We will delve into stories of runners who have forged remarkable paths through their dedication, resilience, and a spirit of celebration. By reflecting on our achievements, we foster gratitude, motivation, and a sense of community, ultimately enriching our experiences as both runners and individuals. I encourage you to not lose sight of the statement that people need people, keep the thought close to your heart and it will serve you and others well.

The Importance of Celebration

Celebration is often overlooked in our pursuit of goals and aspirations. We tend to focus on the finish lines, be they races or personal benchmarks, while forgetting the significance of the journey itself. Acknowledging our successes, no matter their scale, is crucial for several reasons:

1. Reinforcement of Positive Behavior: Celebrating achievements reinforces our commitment to our goals. It reminds us of the effort we put in, encouraging us to continue striving for more. By reinforcing positive behavior, we are fueling our commitment and underpinning our intention.

2. Increased Motivation: Recognizing our successes fuels our motivation. It serves as a reminder of what we can achieve and stirs a desire to set new objectives.

3. Enhancement of Self-Confidence: Each celebration builds on our self-confidence. When we acknowledge our capabilities, we cultivate a positive self-image and strengthen belief in our potential.

4. Strengthening Connections: Sharing victories with others fosters a sense of community. We inspire and uplift fellow runners, reinforcing

the idea that we are interconnected in our journey.

5. Cultivating Gratitude: Reflecting on our successes helps us cultivate gratitude. It invites us to appreciate not only the outcomes but also the challenges and learning opportunities we encountered along the way.

Recognizing All Achievements: Big and Small

As we embark on a journey of celebration, it becomes increasingly important to recognize that every achievement, regardless of its size, deserves acknowledgment. Each run, each milestone reached, contributes to our overall growth and success. Even on days when we feel we fell short, look for the small wins, if nothing else celebrate the fact that we continue to put ourselves our there, we continue to turn up and we continue to work our mind in tandem with our body to connect the mind with the miles and reinforce our intention.

Running Milestones: For some, completing a marathon may be the ultimate achievement, but the journey toward that goal is filled with smaller victories. Whether it's running a personal best in a 5K, successfully completing a long training run, or mastering hill sprints, every accomplishment matters.

Personal Triumphs: Beyond the running context, personal achievements should also be acknowledged. Overcoming mental barriers such as self-doubt or anxiety during training can be as significant as finishing a race. Coping with life's challenges while maintaining a commitment to running is a testament to our strength and dedication.

Consider the story of Sarah, who decided to become a runner to cope with a major life transition. Her journey began with a single step on the treadmill, where she struggled to run for even a minute without stopping. Instead of focusing solely on the length of time she could run, Sarah celebrated every achievement along the way—each minute spent running, every successful week of training, and eventually completing her first 5K. To her, each step represented more than just physical improvement; it symbolized her resilience and determination.

Personal Reflections: Journaling Your Journey

One of the most rewarding ways to celebrate successes is to document our journey. Journaling provides a space for reflection, allowing us to immerse ourselves in our thoughts and feelings about our achievements. This practice can help us articulate our victories and honor our growth.

Creating a running journal can take many forms:

1. Daily Logs: Document your daily runs, noting distances, times, and how you felt. Include your thoughts on what you learned from each session or how it contributed to your goals. This is more than synchronizing your watch or phone with an app, this is honesty, vulnerability, feeling. This level of authenticity is where the real growth occurs.

2. Highlight Achievements: Dedicate sections to listing achievements, be they small or large. Write about the emotions you felt when reaching each milestone and how it impacted your overall journey.

3. Reflective Prompts: At the end of each week or month, set aside time for reflective writing. Consider prompts such as:

    • What achievements am I most proud of this month?

    • What challenges have I overcome, and how have they contributed to my growth?

    • How can I continue to celebrate my journey moving forward?

Through journaling, stories emerge that capture our commitments, struggles, and successes in ways that remind us of how far we have come. Mia, a runner who maintained a journal throughout her training, detailed her experiences—from the initial nervousness before her first race to crossing the finish line with tears of joy. By revisiting her journal entries, she felt inspired and motivated to set new goals, solidifying the impact of recognizing her achievements.

Sharing Successes with Others

Celebration becomes even more meaningful when shared with others. Engaging with fellow runners or friends not only enhances the joy of the moment but also fosters a supportive community that uplifts and motivates us all.

Consider the power of social media in today's interconnected world. Many runners share their training journeys, races, and milestones on platforms like Instagram or Facebook. Posting pictures, videos, or updates about one's accomplishments not only invites encouragement from friends and family but also inspires others to pursue their own running goals.

John transformed his running journey by creating an online community through his blog, where he chronicled his struggles with injuries and how he celebrated each comeback. His transparency resonated with others, and soon readers began sharing their own stories of triumphs alongside his. The motivating energy exchanged created an environment of celebration that enriched everyone involved.

Local running groups also offer fantastic avenues for celebrating success together. Whether it's organizing post-race gatherings or sharing personal achievements during training sessions, fostering camaraderie reinforces connections and encourages continued growth. As members share their accomplishments, completing distance goals, achieving personal bests, or overcoming life challenges, they contribute to a culture of celebration and support.

Setting New Goals: From Achievements to Aspirations

November is not merely a time to reflect on past successes; it also invites us to contemplate future aspirations. Celebrating achievements paves the way for new goals and ambitions. Each milestone reached can serve as a launching pad for further pursuits, providing us with a template for growth. On a personal level my hopes for the year ahead almost always start to come to me in November and I spend the following days and weeks reconciling with the person and runner I am becoming before committing them with intention for the year ahead.

As you reflect on the past year, think about what you learned from your journey, both in terms of running and personal growth. What goals do you wish to set for yourself moving forward? Consider the following approaches to goal setting:

1. SMART Goals: Make your goals Specific, Measurable, Achievable, Relevant, and Time-bound. For example, instead of aiming to "run more," set a goal to run three times a week for a month or run twice for at least 20minutes in the next week. Remember all these goals should be part of an overall picture and not absolute in isolation.

2. Long-Term vs. Short-Term Goals: Balance immediate and long-term goals. Short-term goals help maintain motivation, while long-term goals give you a vision to strive toward. One of my favorite phrases is that there is no point planning for summer if you can't make it through winter. In that I mean, there is no point having a big audacious goal if you don't have milestones along the way that will align your mental health with your physical capability and ensure that you connect the miles with the mind. Reflect on what you hope to accomplish by next November, be it a certain race, a new personal record, or improving your physical and mental health.

3. Personal Growth Goals: In addition to running-specific goals, consider personal development as part of your journey. This could include improving nutrition, working on mental resilience, or participating in community events. Personal growth complements your physical training and enhances your overall well-being.

Lily, an experienced runner, took time in November to reflect on her accomplishments over the past season. After completing her first marathon, she set her sights on a new goal: to diversify her running experience by participating in different types of races. Instead of focusing solely on distance, she sought to challenge herself with trail runs, races in different terrains, and even obstacle courses.

Her reflections led to an exciting mix of aspirations, creating a comprehensive vision of growth for the upcoming year. By setting both performance-based goals and personal development goals, Lily solidified her commitment to pursuing diverse opportunities. She not only became more resilient, but she also started to build grit, felt a better balance in her life and showed more gratitude for the simple things that came her way.

Embracing the Journey, Not Just the Destination

In the rush to celebrate achievements, it is vital to remember that the journey is as significant as the conclusions. Running encompasses not only the moments of success but also the struggles, sacrifices, and growth experienced along the way. Embracing the journey allows us to appreciate the beauty in the process itself.

Erica learned this lesson as she prepared for her first half marathon. In the months leading up to race day, she faced injuries, self-doubt, and daunting training runs. While crossing the finish line was rewarding, the moments leading up to it—the missed workouts, the daily battles with her inner critic, and the unwavering support of a training partner—defined her journey.

She found joy in sharing these stories with other runners. By embracing the lessons learned through challenges, Erica became more than just a finisher; she became an ambassador for persistence and determination. Her story resonated, encouraging others to find strength in their struggles and reminding them that every setback is an opportunity for growth.

Recognizing the importance of the journey fosters an appreciation for every step taken, whether it's the exhilarating highs or the challenging lows. As we move through November, allow yourself to embrace both the celebration and the complexity of your experiences.

Gratitude and Reflection

As we approach the end of the year, November serves not only as a month for celebrating successes but also as a month for gratitude and reflection. This season invites us to express appreciation for what we have accomplished and those who have supported us along the way.

Gratitude practices can significantly enhance our emotional well-being. During this month, consider making a conscious effort to acknowledge the people who have made a positive impact on your running journey. This could be a friend who trained alongside you, a coach who provided guidance, or family members who cheered you on during races.

Writing gratitude letters can be a meaningful way to express your appreciation. Take the initiative to reach out to those who have encouraged you, explaining how their support has influenced your journey. Sharing these sentiments strengthens relationships and reminds us of the interconnectedness of our experiences. I am convinced that it is also good for your spirit and nourishes your soul.

Conclusion:
Celebrating Successes Together

As November draws to a close, let us commit to celebrating our successes, both big and small, throughout our running journeys. Each mile, each accomplishment, each lesson learned deserves recognition and appreciation. By fostering a culture of celebration, we inspire not only ourselves but also those around us.

Reflect on your achievements, take note of the resilience you've built, and honor the journey that has brought you to this moment. Embrace the joy of sharing your successes with others, allowing your triumphs to motivate and uplift the community of fellow runners.

As we enter the final weeks of the year, remember that celebration is not merely a fleeting moment but an ongoing practice that informs our mindsets and enriches our experiences. Carry the spirit of celebration into the upcoming year, and let it serve as a guide as you face new challenges, aspire for new goals, and continue your journey as a runner and individual. Embed this celebration and gratitude into your meditation practice and find space for it in your mantras.

November invites you not just to celebrate the successes you have achieved but to look forward, with hope and determination, to the successes yet to come. Each step you take is an opportunity to grow, learn, and inspire others on their own journeys. So, lace up your shoes, reflect on your path, and embrace the joy of celebrating every success, one stride at a time. Take time to double down on understanding your why and this will bring your mind closer to your miles with each intentional step.

Call to Action: Celebrate the Miles, Ignite the Fire

Take this moment, this breath of November and hold it close, you have earned it. Every early alarm. Every aching stride. Every I did not think I could, but I did.
Now celebrate it. Loudly or quietly. Publicly or privately. But honestly. Because this journey, your journey, deserves recognition.

- Big wins. Quiet victories.
- The days you soared. The days you just showed up.
- The detours that became defining moments.

Don't downplay your story. Own it. Share it. Stand tall in it, and then, when the confetti settles and the gratitude flows, ask yourself what is next?
You are not just reflecting. You are fueling your next goal. Celebrate your success like a spark, then light the torch for the road ahead.

Stride into your next season with joy, pride, and a heart wide open. The best victories are still waiting. There will be more of them than ever before with new people to share them with from your ever-expanding community, the best part is you get to share in their victories too. Reflect, replenish, nourish the soul and spirit and start to look forward to the new year. However, first a chance to close out the year by refocusing on gratitude, authenticity, intention and purpose. December here we come.

RUNNING INTO THE FUTURE

Setting intentions for the coming year and the lifelong journey of running.

DECEMBER

Chapter 12:

DECEMBER

Running onto the future. Setting intentions for the coming year and your lifelong journey of running

Seasonal Reflection:

The year concludes with a time for reflection amidst the holiday season. Invite a sense of closure and renewal as you consider all you've experienced.

Mindfulness Theme:

Meditate on the lessons learned over the year. Your runs can become a ceremonial act of gratitude, allowing thoughts of growth and hope to flourish as you welcome the New Year.

Mental Health Insight:

The end of the year can bring feelings of pressure and anxiety. Utilize your running practice as a form of self-care, focusing on mental wellness, compassion, and setting intentions for the upcoming year.

December Mantra:

"I run with vision. I set intentions in motion. My future is built one stride at a time."

Running into the Future

As the final month of the year descends, December invites us to reflect on the past while simultaneously casting our gaze towards the future. With the holidays approaching, it's a season adorned with joy, gratitude, and the promise of new beginnings. In the realm of running, December presents a significant opportunity to set intentions that will shape our journey in the upcoming year. It's a time for reflection, goal setting, and mapping out a path that honors our love for running and our connection to ourselves.

In the following pages, we will explore the key elements of setting intentions for the coming year while considering the lifelong journey of running. As we delve into personal stories, practical tips, and inspirational insights, we will uncover how to transform aspirations into actionable steps that shape our future as runners and individuals and help to balance our mental health by connecting our mind with the miles.

The Intentional Journey: Why Set Intentions?

Setting intentions is more than simply outlining goals, it's about cultivating a mindset that guides our actions and decisions. Intentions arise from a place of mindfulness and self-awareness, allowing us to focus on what truly matters to us. By establishing clear intentions for the upcoming year, we create a roadmap that aligns our running journey with our values, passions, and aspirations.

1. Clarity of Purpose: Intentions provide clarity on our motivations. They allow us to define what running means to us, whether it's competition, personal growth, mental well-being, or community connection.

2. Direction: Intentions act as a compass that guides our actions. They help us make choices that align with our aspirations and steer clear of distractions that can derail our progress.

3. Empowerment: Setting intentions empowers us to take ownership of our experiences. It transforms the running journey into a proactive pursuit rather than a passive one, inspiring us to continually grow and evolve. Stating our intention gives us permission to participate and execute against our goals.

4. Mindfulness: Intentions encourage us to be present in our experiences. Rather than merely chasing outcomes, we learn to appreciate the process of running, cultivating gratitude for each step taken.

5. Flexibility: While goals may be specific and measurable, intentions can be more fluid,

allowing for adaptability. Life is unpredictable, and intentions remind us to embrace change and stay open to new opportunities. We can still find a reason to celebrate the small wins, even if we need to adjust our overall direction from time to time.

Reflecting on the Past Year

Before we can effectively set intentions for the coming year, it's essential to reflect on the past year. Taking time to assess what went well, what challenges you faced, and how you grew as a runner and a person and determining how your mental health held up on that journey helps to establish a foundation for your intentions.

Journaling Reflection: Consider dedicating a session to journaling about your running experiences over the past year. You might start with prompts such as:

- What were my proudest achievements in running this year?
- What challenges did I encounter, and what did I learn from them?
- How have I grown as a runner and as a person through my experiences?
- What moments brought me the most joy and fulfillment?

- How has your mental health changed over the past year? Which tools have been the most effective?

For example, Mark, an avid runner, took the time to reflect on his year. He discovered that despite setbacks from injuries, he had completed his first ultra-marathon and had cultivated new friendships within a running community. Mark realized that his ability to adapt and persevere was more significant than any single race result. This insight became the foundation of his intentions moving forward as well as giving him the confidence to grow his community which in turn had significant positive impact on his mental health.

Reflecting on our journey allows us to appreciate the highs and lows, reminding us that both are essential components of our physical, mental and spiritual development. Celebrate the successes while graciously acknowledging the challenges, they contribute to the fabric of who we are as runners and individuals.

Goal setting: From Intentions to Actionable Steps

Once you've reflected on the past year, it's time to translate your insights into actionable steps for the future. Setting measurable goals guided by your intentions ensures you create a clear path toward what you want to achieve. As we have explored in previous sections of the book, the SMART criteria, Specific, Measurable, Achievable, Relevant, and time-bound, can be an excellent framework for developing your goals.

Consider the example of Jenna, who wanted to improve her 5K time. Reflecting on her past year, she recognized she had been consistent in her training but needed a more structured approach. With the SMART criteria, she set a goal to run the local 5K in March, aiming to complete it in under 25 minutes. Her training plan included interval workouts, strength training, and nutrition strategies, helping her stay focused and motivated as she approached her goal.

Intentions for Holistic Growth

While setting specific running goals is essential, don't overlook the breadth of your overall well-being. Incorporating intentions focused on mental, emotional, and social aspects of your life enriches your journey as a runner. Consider the following areas:

1. Mental Health: Intend to prioritize mental well-being through mindfulness practices. Consider incorporating meditation, yoga, or breathing exercises into your routine to enhance your focus and relaxation.

2. Emotional Resilience: Reflect on ways to build emotional resilience. Set intentions to approach challenges with a positive mindset and embrace failures as opportunities to learn. Develop strategies and processes that allow calmness and thought over being overly emotive and irrational.

3. Community Engagement: Establish intentions to foster connections within the running community. Engage with local running groups, participate in charity events, or mentor aspiring runners. Building relationships enriches your journey and creates lasting bonds. Remember that our true value and a good measure of authenticity is not what we know or even what we say but what we do.

4. Self-Care: Prioritize self-care practices that go beyond running. Intend to establish nourishing habits, such as regular massages, stretching routines, or time set aside for hobbies that bring you joy.

5. Lifelong Learning: Embrace a growth mindset by committing to lifelong learning in your running journey. This could include reading books or articles on running techniques, attending workshops, or engaging with running coaches.

As Jerry contemplated his intentions, he realized he wanted to enhance his mental stamina while running long races. He decided to focus on integrating mindful running practices into his training—by setting intentions to practice gratitude during runs and embrace the beauty of the moment. This intention transformed his perspective, allowing him to appreciate every step rather than fixating solely on pace.

Creating a Vision Board

Visual representation of your intentions can serve as a powerful motivator as you move into the new year. Creating a vision board allows you to visualize your goals and aspirations, making them more tangible in your mind.

1. Gather Materials: Gather magazines, photos, quotes, and any visual elements that resonate with your intentions and goals for the year ahead.

2. Reflect and Organize: As you create your vision board, consider how each visual element aligns with your aspirations. Consider sections for running-specific goals, personal growth, and community engagement.

3. Display Your Board: Once you have your board assembled, place it somewhere visible—a

reminder of what you are working toward. Allow it to inspire you daily as you embark on your journey in the coming year.

Anna, a dedicated runner and teacher, found immense joy in creating an annual vision board. This year, she mapped out her running aspirations alongside personal intentions related to work-life balance and family connections. Having her vision board in her home office gave her a daily reminder of her purpose, motivating her to stay focused on her goals as she approached the new year.

Embracing Change: The Lifelong Journey of Running

Running is more than just a sport; it's a lifelong journey filled with ups, downs, and countless discoveries. Embracing the idea that running evolves and adapts with us fosters resilience and a healthy relationship with the sport.

Recognize that the path ahead may present unexpected challenges—injuries, schedule changes, habits that may need reassessment. During these times, self-compassion becomes crucial. Understand that every runner faces obstacles and that it's normal for the journey to deviate.

When faced with setbacks, take a moment to adjust your intentions. This flexibility demonstrates strength and adaptability. Embrace the belief that progress isn't linear and requires patience and perseverance. Take the time to listen to your body and revise your plans as needed.

Jessica experienced this firsthand when she suffered a minor injury halfway through her training plan for a spring marathon. Instead of letting disappointment consume her, she reframed her intentions, focusing on rehabilitation and cross-training. By adjusting her goals and maintaining a positive mindset, she emerged stronger, ultimately finding success in a different race a few months later.

Building Your Support Network

Running is often perceived as a solitary sport, but the reality is that community plays a vital role in our success and enjoyment. Emphasizing relationships with fellow runners, coaches, friends, and family creates a network of support that enhances your running experience.

Consider taking steps to nurture your support network in the coming year:

1. Find a Running Buddy: Seek out a training partner who shares similar goals. Running with someone can increase accountability and make workouts more enjoyable.

2. Join a Local Running Group: Explore local running clubs or groups in your area. Engaging with a community of like-minded individuals fosters camaraderie and provides motivation during challenging times.

3. Offer Support: Celebrate the successes of fellow runners as much as you celebrate your own. Offering words of encouragement and support creates an empowering environment for all involved.

4. Seek Guidance: Connect with experienced runners or coaches who can offer insights and guidance tailored to your goals. Mentorship can be invaluable as you navigate your running journey.

5. Stay Connected: Use social media and online platforms to connect with a broader community of runners. Sharing experiences, challenges, and successes online can inspire and uplift everyone involved.

Mark forged lasting friendships with fellow runners in his local community through a running club. Together, they celebrated each other's milestones while also navigating the challenges of training. This support system became integral to his journey, enhancing the joy of running and helping him stay accountable to his intentions.

Conclusion: Running into the Future

As we close the chapter on another year, December signifies a time for intention-setting, reflection, and growth. By taking the time to assess our journeys, acknowledge our accomplishments, and establish intentions for the future, we can create a meaningful path as runners and individuals, we can create a path filled with physical and mental balance, integrity and authenticity.

Let this December be a catalyst for transformation as you embrace the upcoming year with enthusiasm and purpose. Carry the lessons learned, the connections forged, and the joy of running into everything you pursue. Remember that the running journey is lifelong—one that evolves and adapts as we do.

As you lace up your shoes, allow your intentions to guide your steps; let gratitude and mindfulness accompany you on every run. Each stride brings new opportunities and experiences, and with every mile, you weave the narrative of your life as a runner.

May this chapter of your journey inspire growth, connection, and resilience, propelling you forward into a bright future filled with possibilities. The road ahead is expansive, and with intentionality, you can run into the future with confidence, joy, and determination.

Your Call to Action: Run Forward with Intention

As December ends, take a moment to honor how far you've come. Now, it's time to look ahead with clarity, courage, and heart.

- What do you want your running story to say next year?
- What kind of runner, and person, are you becoming?

Before you turn the page into a new year, I invite you to pause and act, if you follow the actions below, we can look forward to the running adventures ahead of us with commitment, intention and joy.

Set three intentions for your running journey in the new year. Let them reflect your values, your joy, and your aspirations, not just your mileage.

Reflect on your biggest lesson from the past year. Write it down, carry it with you, and let it be your compass when the road gets rough.

Create your vision board, journal entry, or mantra for the year ahead—whatever speaks to your soul. Make it real. Make it visible.

Most importantly, commit to yourself, not just as a runner, but as someone worthy of growth, celebration, and second chances.

Remember, you are not just running into a new year, you are running **into a future shaped by intention.** And that? That is without doubt one of the most powerful strides that you can take.

So, I say to you once again, lace up, lean in, and run forward. Your future is waiting. And it's going to be brilliant.